Bipolar Love

Caring for the Caregiver

8 Simple Steps

To Self-Care

S R John

Book ISBN: 978-1-7772433-2-6
Electronic ISBN: 978-1-7772433-3-3
Hardcover ISBN: 978-1-7772433-4-0

ACKNOWLEDGEMENT

I am nothing without the people in my life who have brought me to where I am today. To my kid, I love you and it is an honour and a privilege to share my life with you. You always keep me moving forward. We have shared a lot and there are more wonderful experiences awaiting us. To my special friend who has always had my back. Thank you for being you.

To all who read this. Life is a journey for us to discover which way we want to go and only we will know the destination. Don't get lost. Take the time to enjoy the masterpiece of your life. Love will always show you the way.

S.R. John

Table of Contents

Chapter One
Introduction
Caring for the Caregiver

Welcome to Bipolar Love, Caring for the Caregiver, 8 Simple Steps To Self-Care. As caregivers, we often forget to look after ourselves when we are caring for those we love. For many years, I looked after my ex-husband who was diagnosed with a mental illness, and years later looked after a parent, who had suffered a major life-altering illness. It took me years to realize I was making myself sick as I pushed through my days in both situations. But I had people who depended on me. So, I did what I had to do until I could not continue in the capacity that I had in the past. I eventually realized I had to make some changes to keep myself healthy and sane through all that I was going through.

Taking care of someone that is not well can be exhausting and it doesn't matter if you are taking care of someone for a short time or a long time. It can be for a mental illness, looking after seniors, or for many other reasons. As difficult as the ailments are for those experiencing health issues, looking after them takes a toll on the caregivers' emotions and how their health and lives change, depending on the experiences and how situations are handled.

Self-love is not easy. There are so many things that can take up your time and attention and when do you stop and take a much-needed moment for yourself? Without feeling guilty about it. Or before you become so ill, that you just cannot function the way you used to in the past? Sometimes we think that the things we did when we were much younger can still be accomplished when we are much older and, in most cases, we cannot. Our bodies naturally age and the things we do to them also change us. But that doesn't mean we can't stay strong and healthy. We can by paying attention to our bodies and our needs, then doing what we must to stay that way. We may jump back to our old ways from time to time, but it's recognizing that we have to make a change for the better and following through.

Among many other things, stress, worry, overworking yourself, lack of sleep, and trying to juggle more things than your body and mind want to handle, will begin to affect your way of life and you must remember to take a step back when things get too hectic. Most of us, me included just keep on moving along, not realizing the damage we are doing to ourselves until one day we wake up and can't move or discover various illnesses that have slowly crept upon us. If we are lucky, it may just be a few wrinkles and some grey hair.

We hear our family and friends, even doctors telling us to slow down and change our way of living to stay healthy and heal what needs our love. But we don't listen. How many times have you been told that sleep helps the healing process? So why do we keep pushing our beautiful bodies that wake us up every morning and keep us moving? Why do we wait until something has gone wrong and we feel more aches and pains, like the tummy that doesn't feel well or the constant headaches we get when we don't normally suffer from them? And if we don't hear what our bodies are trying to tell us, we can end up with bigger problems like the pain in our chest that needs immediate attention. Disease will find us if we are not listening.

There are so many concerns when we are caring for someone else. It's not just the physical part of looking after them, but there are other things to think about too. Even worrying about money can keep you awake at night and thinking about how you are going to pay for all the changes you must make in your lives. Maybe there were two incomes before and now there is only one. There may be children at home who need your attention, but your time is split between looking after them, and your loved ones who are not well. So, do you keep the children at home with you, to save money, but can't provide them the much-needed attention? Or bring them to daycare, so you can concentrate on looking after your loved ones that need a different kind of attention. There may be equipment and supplies to buy, maybe even modifications to a room or the house. Ramps may need to be put in for wheelchair accessibility and finding the right caregivers to give you a hand if you need it.

When do you stop thinking about what needs to be done today, tomorrow, or next week? You are taking care of someone you love so your time is not your own. To add to the equation, your partner needs you, your kids need you, and your friends and others in your lives may want a piece of you too. Plus, there are plans to make, like maybe a career to think about, work, your business and maybe other hired help that are not doing what you ask of them or better put, how you are accustomed to doing things. So, you may find yourselves retracing their steps.

There are also a handful of many other things that can throw you off your game. Just these past few years with the pandemic changing the way we have all had to live has thrown a wrench into many people's lives and in some cases, tight quarters have become even tighter. Some have been working from home and many have added to their roles of educating and parenting their children as well as caregiving duties, all while juggling the extra meals and chores with everybody home. Not to mention that things like water and electricity bills probably had a big increase. It is all stressful.

It can be enough to let you want to pull out your hair. And indeed, some people may even begin to lose theirs and don't even realize it's all the stress they are under that is causing their bodies to react in different ways. So, you try and put some rules in place in hopes of getting balance in your world. But life is fluid. You cannot structure it, try as you might control it. You need to move with it as best you can so that you have an easier time coping with the events life throws your way.

For the most part, you may have a routine that works for you while taking care of everyone plus, those that need more attention. So, you go about your days, and all is working like a well-oiled machine. But then something happens and your day changes. Maybe your loved ones need more attention than normal, and you have to stop what you are doing and tend to them. You have hired help to assist with your caregiving needs and they do not show up and this was supposed to be the day you rest or have an important appointment to attend. Or the clothes did not get washed on Wednesday and the house did not get cleaned on Saturday. And darn it, the sink is full of everybody else's dishes. And the worst is that you know everyone is waiting on you to do them.

You try and get back to that routine, but everything has changed and now you are having a hard time coping with whatever is going on. The one thing not to do is panic, not to freak out, not to yell and scream and blame your children, your spouse or partner, your loved one who is not well, the Universe, God, or whomever you are directing your anger to, because that alone is sucking up your energy and will leave you so exhausted that now you have even less energy than before. Plus, you may hate yourself later for upsetting those you love.

It is ok if things have changed. That is going to happen in life. As difficult as it can be at times, we have to adjust our days with whatever comes our way and keep a level head. That will help us to make sound decisions and better our situations. We also do not want to upset everyone else around us, because you know it can come back to bit us. Yes, some days and maybe some weeks, if not months will be difficult to adapt to what is going on and you wonder when it will all end. There will be an outcome, one way or another, so you have to work at making that time as easy for yourself as you possibly can. That of course, will be different in every situation.

When I say not to freak out, it is ok to release your frustrations, so you do not bottle them up. We are only human after all, just work at not directing that anger to others so you do not add more upset to your day or theirs. Let the little things go as well because some things cannot be changed. Do not try and control your life too much. You have to let go of the reins sometimes and go with the flow. Just allow the day to unfold because what is going to happen is going to happen. As I said, you can not change some outcomes.

The best way I found that helped me to keep a level head when everything was crumbling around me, was to stay as calm as I could, take a few extra deep breaths, and step away from a situation that was getting too much to handle. Sometimes I would stare in the mirror at the person looking back at me and wonder how I was going to get through the difficult times I was experiencing. Not only when dealing with my ex-husband's emotional ups and downs but also, later with my ill parent as I tried to heal my own body. There was little support, and the situations were wearing me down.

But we have to preserver if we are going to get through whatever challenges we are facing at this moment or the next. If you give up, I don't have to tell you that things can get harder, so keep moving forward. Look for assistance if something is too difficult to do on your own. You'd be surprised how many people you can find that do care.

Try not to get caught up in other people's angry rants, worries, or concerns that have nothing to do with you. I know this can be difficult sometimes when you want to be there for your family, friends, or those you love. And sometimes you may be needed as a mediator. Especially in family squabbles, but you don't want to add any more drama to your life if you can avoid it. You are already coping with a lot. Try not to get involved too deeply, in other people's problems that are going to drain you. Not to mention, that sometimes others need to learn some life lessons and you keeping your distance will allow them to experience those.

Sometimes family can get upset because you are not able to give them your full, undivided attention. Or they may not approve of how you are caring for a loved one. I have had my fair share of squabbles as most people do and have had to hold my ground many times and I learned to set my boundaries better. Something I did not do well in the past.

Remember, we all go through things with our loved ones and every situation is a chance to improve what we did not like or thought we could do differently. For me, I'm still learning, growing, tweaking what I want to see differently or better in my life, so I am more aware now of when I need to stop and look after myself if I know I've done too much.

It isn't easy to break away when someone needs you or expects something more of you than you can give. But when you need to take a break it's a good idea to listen to your body and do so. I have gone for many walks, and it helped me to calm down from whatever was going on and recharge my batteries. I know you can't always just get up and leave, but the moment you can, go.

Relieve that stress you are feeling and take that important downtime. Work on your mental and physical health which gets stretched beyond what is healthy. Learn to adapt to situations and work things out as best you can. I know some days you may not know where to turn. But don't give up, you will work things out one way or another.

Adapting to a situation may look different for everyone and may not work for some since we all have our ways of handling things. So, you may have to find what works best for you. Maybe it's leaving a situation entirely. But if you cannot because you have people depending on you, and you are beginning to feel the stress or someone is upsetting you, then look for ways to relieve that stress, otherwise, you will find yourself getting overwhelmed, emotionally sick, maybe angry at people you love, and unable to cope with even bigger issues now, which can land you in the hospital if things get really bad.

There are some quick things you can do on the spot to calm yourself down which I'm sure you have heard of but may not remember. Counting down, backward, or reciting a special verse to find your moment of peace can help. You can take a break and call on a trusted friend who can lend an ear or give you some sound advice. If you are juggling too much, then look at bringing in some outside help if you can. Listen to some music you love or do something that makes you happy. Take a walk in nature, read, write, paint.

There are so many other ways to find your centre of peace again. Losing your cool only wastes time to get to the next step in fixing whatever is not going your way and as mentioned, stresses you out, which in turn plants just another seed that will grow and grow into disease. I have shared a few other things later in the chapters that I did that helped me and others I know to release some of the anxiety and feelings of stress.

If you are at work or handling a personal project and something goes wrong, you immediately take steps to correct the situation. Maybe you are building a deck or fixing a car. Learning a new recipe that didn't come out the way you expected. You may step away to re-evaluate how to fix things, then maybe contact others that can help you work out the problem together. If you sit there and complain or play the victim or wait until someone else fixes the situation, nothing will change. Then you end up in deeper trouble or not getting the results you are looking for and you end up hating where you are at and again, stressed out even more than before.

Caring for our loved ones is no different in the sense that sometimes we need to take a step back and look at things another way. We may need to involve others in our plan or change things somehow. What that is will depend on what is going on and the changes you are ready or willing to make. But you must take the first step and realize things are getting too heavy for you to handle alone and begin to involve others to give you a hand.

Don't try to measure up to the expectations others have of you either and don't be so hard on yourself. Looking after your family is a big job on its own. Now add to that, caring for someone that desperately needs your help, in whatever capacity that is. So be there for them, but also make sure to look after yourself. And if it does not happen today, because something changed, maybe tomorrow will be better. Just try not to keep putting it off. If you have to call in others to give you a much-needed break, do it, because it will help you to recharge your strength and you can look at another day with optimism, instead of despair.

I know how difficult it can be to stop and look after ourselves when we are juggling so much in life. It was well into my marriage when my ex-husband was diagnosed with Bipolar, and every day was a challenge as I worked at trying to calm his emotional turmoil. Eventually, he became a danger to be around, and life changed for us all. Most recently when I was caring for my ill parent after their life-changing health crisis, they needed more attention than what I could physically give. It was a trying time, but I managed to survive with my mental sanity somewhat intact. I say somewhat because as I mentioned earlier, caregiving takes its toll on us all and some can not understand what we go through unless they are in the thick of it themselves so we may be handling a lot more than we bargained for on our own.

For me, I continued to push through the days as I cared for those I loved until I, myself ended up with health issues. There were things that as the wife, the daughter, the person put in the positions I was in as I looked after those I loved, were expected of me from family. As well as things I believed I should do in my roles, without any thought to what I was doing to my health. I wish I knew then what I know today about self-love, self-care, boundaries, standing up for myself, and speaking my truth. As well as giving myself time to adjust to new situations instead of trying to make things work the old way because that was just the way it was always done.

I did not open to change or extend a hand for some help. I believed things had to be a certain way, because of my upbringing. So, I just tried to juggle everything myself. The worst belief was thinking that nobody would be available to want to help me care for someone with a mental disposition. That was further than the truth. I just did not know where to turn for help or maybe I was too exhausted to think straight after dealing with my ex-husband's emotional ups and downs for so long. So, I just kept going, changing nothing, since what I was doing seemed to be working for me. Or was it. I was slowly making myself sick and did not realize how detrimental my situation was until years later.

It was a big mistake not reaching out for help, but I also did not want others to know what was going on in my world, for fear of being labeled, or others not wanting to socialize with me and my family. I did not want to look weak in the eyes of others, or incapable of handling the stuff that came my way. Nor did I wish to give others a reason to judge me for making the choices that I did in my life.

I was raised in a strict European household, so there was no room for error, no room for changing the old ways, or thinking differently, and if you did you were on your own, maybe outcast, so basically, it was one of those things where you were expected to suck it up, follow the rules and deal with whatever was going on. Let's put it this way, back then, if you married and realized, this was not the one, you did not ask for a divorce. You worked it out. You married them; you were expected to put up with the situation. The belief was that society and even some religions would not look well on you as divorce was still not an acceptable thing to do. In some cases, I knew about, this affected women more than men. Unfortunately, in some cultures, this may still be the case where the women are expected to obey the men, and they have little say in their world.

Things are more acceptable today in most circles, but back then, in some of our cultures, there was no crying or feeling sorry for yourself If someone was not well, you were expected to look after them, and it didn't matter if it was driving you off the deep end or making you physically sick. You did not look to psychiatrists who could help you cope with what you were going through, never mind what your loved one was experiencing. That just was not the way back then in some circles. Because not only was that admitting to a weakness, but it cost money. Money that would take away from caring for your family.

There would be no weakness shown here and no pity or help if you chose another route. And if you left the situation or put your loved ones in an institution, oh boy, you were considered the worst person on this earth. It was just unfathomable to do such a thing. But as I said, nobody knows the truth of what everyone is experiencing, except those going through the ordeal. Nobody knows the lack of sleep you are getting as you tend to your loved ones. Nobody knows the abuse you put your body through as you lift or move someone from a bed to a wheelchair or deal with someone who through no fault of their own may be violent, given their state of mind, maybe having Dementia, Alzheimer's or other illnesses. And nobody knows your health issues and what you can mentally and physically handle.

Recently, at a nursing home visiting family, someone I was with noticed a European woman that the family knew, and they innocently asked if she was there for her mother. She denied the truth, telling us she was there just visiting a friend, and quickly rushed off. Well, we were in the middle of this world pandemic still, so she certainly was not there to visit a friend. The nursing home would not have let her even close to anyone other than her immediate family and only if she was designated as the family caregiver would she have access to anyone inside. The nursing home still had very strict rules for outsiders. Shortly after, we saw her pushing her mother around in a wheelchair and she tried hard to avoid us, but there was no other path she could take as we too sat with our own family in a common area.

Maybe she felt guilty for not being able to care for her mother herself or thought others would look down upon her for putting a family member in an institution. Regardless of the reason, she felt she had to justify her actions, lying about the truth. My heart went out to her because I knew how difficult a decision it must have been, having experienced the same thing ourselves. But sometimes, as much as you don't want to do it, it may be the best place to give your loved ones the care they need. This woman was well into her 70's and had health issues of her own and given the condition we saw her mother in, it would probably be difficult to care for her at home. We did not, nor would we judge caring for someone in whatever way works best for everyone involved. It's a tough job and you certainly have to be up for the challenge, mentally and physically.

For me, I did the best I could with the cards I guess I had dealt for myself, given that we all have choices, but I kept getting up, dusting myself off, and going at life again, the next day and the next. Sometimes it is not easy trying to fit into everybody else's shoes but your own.

As caregivers there is a love and a duty, to care for those we love with all our hearts and with all the strength we can muster. We are a special breed, not realizing the strength we have, mentally and physically. Not everyone is designed to take on this task. We wake up every day ready to take on what comes our way, already exhausted from the day before, or the many sleepless nights and stress we put ourselves through, without any thought to what is happening to our bodies and how the situation affects us mentally and physically.

Many of us get caregiver burnout. We do not take the time to sleep or eat right and stop looking after our own needs. Our exhaustion can among other things, give us headaches, make us irritable, and we can begin to argue with the person we are caring for or others because we just cannot focus anymore. It is easy to feel resentment towards many and depression as well as other ailments can set in when our resistance is low and if we are not careful, we will be the ones who will soon need a caregiver to look after us.

We need to take care of ourselves before we get to this point, because if our health suffers, it may be hard to get back to the health we had before we became a caregiver. Not to mention that we cannot be there to look after those we love, because of our declining health.

Sometimes it just takes us realizing and accepting that we are beginning to burn out and then changing the way we do things to protect ourselves from getting sick. These things may be common sense, but we forget or do not think of them because we get so caught up in our lives of looking after our loved ones and everything else, we have to do in a day. If we take a moment and breathe... if we just stop.... close our eyes and take another breath, we may realize there are things we can do to make our life easier and enjoy it.

When I was with my ex-husband, my days were full of looking after him and his roller coaster of emotions. His mental instability gave me my own emotions to deal with, and there were many. I had to keep him happy and calm as well as not give him too much to deal with, removing any stressful situations. There were days when this could be a challenge as I did not have a crystal ball to predict events that could affect his mood swings. I was no expert in mental illness, so I did what I could in hopes that his moods would not decline through the days, months, and years.

My ex-husband was great at masking his emotions so there were many times I would not know how bad he was feeling, then one day he asked me to hide his medications because he was suicidal. As much as I tried to keep a close eye on him and his changing moods, I had no idea his emotional state had declined so much. I feared for his life and my family's. The mind is a delicate thing, and I did not know what was going on with his thoughts. I could only help him so much, given the knowledge I had on mental illness and available resources.

My ex-husband had never raised a hand to us or threatened us, but when he started to have these negative thoughts and angrier outbursts I knew something more was happening to him. I did not know how else to help him other than bring him to our family doctor or the hospital, depending on how bad he was feeling at any given time. Plus, this situation gave me more things to worry about, adding to an already stressful life.

Attending the doctor's appointments on his own, he would forget to discuss some of the important issues regarding his emotions. Some days he would ask me to write down the points he wanted to discuss but then forgetting that note in his pocket. Still, he would insist on going to the appointments on his own. This became worrisome and frustrating because with his symptoms not getting addressed, he would ultimately end up back at the doctor's office or we would end up at the hospital with him having a difficult time dealing with things.

Unfortunately, as much as privacy laws protect the individual, they also stop us from helping our loved ones further and I was constantly running into roadblocks as I tried to navigate the health system. It was difficult to know the truth as to how bad my ex-husband's symptoms became. If we attended the family doctor together, then I was able to give my input on his situation and we were able to address his needs better. However, if my ex-husband would attend a psychiatrist's office, the few he was lucky enough to see, they would not allow me in the office with them, even though my ex-husband would want me there. As much as I hated it, I understood the doctors wanted to get my ex-husband's perspective on things, but at the same time, it was not helping him heal since he did not know fully, what to discuss with the doctors which in turn would leave his ailments, fears, and emotions unchecked and unbalanced.

I would sit in the waiting room at the hospital for my ex-husband to come back down from the doctor's office and he would return seemingly, happy only to have his emotions come crashing down again, later that day or the next, the talk with the doctor, not helping him much. I began to understand his pattern and knew that if his emotions began to decline and medications were not adjusted, his mental ability to focus could continue spiraling downward. It was like the medications just stopped working and that was exactly what we eventually were told. But we did not learn until years later, that some people could become immune to medications over time.

There was a lot of love in my heart for my ex-husband but dealing with his changing emotions was exhausting and stressful. At times, his actions, confused or frightened me and I continued to run into barriers looking for the right doctors that could help him. All the while hoping we could find that magic remedy that would give me back my husband. He said, did, and thought strange things, that were not the norm for the way society acts. I was constantly making excuses to others about his behavior. I took on the role of wife and caregiver to my ex-husband, and mother and father to our child. I was the person everyone came to for answers, for help and to run the household. I was the person my ex-husband depended on to be there for him, and I made sure I was.

Why did I not see the full picture of what I was getting into? Hindsight is a wonderful thing. When I first met my ex-husband, he did suffer from mild depression, but he was happy for the most part. He was not rude or belligerent. He was not aggressive towards me or others. He was very kind, loving, and caring. I did however realize as time went on, that his extra exuberance was a façade, a way to hide his real emotions.

One of the things that attracted me to my ex-husband was his gentle nature. He was also not the typical male I was used to seeing in my European environment, where the men ruled, and the women were expected to be the domestic housewives, obeying them. My ex-husband helped around the house and in the beginning, we shared our chores, whether it was cutting the grass, washing dishes, or doing laundry. Whoever got to the chore first or preferred one chore over another just did it. There were no arguments.

He had two kids of his own from a previous marriage so I could see the type of father my ex-husband would be to our child when we were ready to have one together. Something we had already discussed. I did not think having depression was a big thing. I figured; everybody has something to deal with. What was a little depression? I never expected his emotions to change so much over the years. Never to the extent they did.

Things were not as bad when it was just, him and me but once our child was born, his attitudes changed. My ex-husband developed jealousy for this newborn which I had heard happens with new parents because your attention is directed more towards the child and a partner may feel left out. So, again, even though some red flags went up for me, for the most part, I did not think much of it, sure this attitude of his would subside. But

I probably was denying what I knew to be true in my heart. That there was something not right with my ex-husband's attitude and emotions. And I am not talking just the normal way in which couples grow and change over a marriage. When you are dealing with a mental illness, it is a whole other ball game.

As time passed and my ex-husband withdrew more and more into himself, most of the family responsibilities fell to me. I had to look after the household, our young baby, and everything else life threw at me. My ex-husband was a good man overall, but when the Bipolar demons got him, he was another person I did not recognize. As difficult as it was for him to experience what he was going through, it was just as hard for me to deal with everything that was thrown my way. Where he was getting some emotional assistance through family doctors, and psychiatrists, I was not. Every day presented a new experience and I had to find a new way to adapt to his ever-changing moods.

In many situations, the caregiver is left to fend for themselves. There is no time to worry about looking after our needs and emotions. We tell ourselves we are good. Better than those we are caring for, so why would we complain when they are going through so much more than us? So, we hold strong and keep burying our emotions and all we are suffering through. We feel there is just too much for us to do to begin looking after ourselves now. It just can't happen. We have to be alert and, on the ball, to catch whatever is going on around us, especially with those we are caring for. But when is it our turn to look after our own needs too? We are also the first ones to get blamed if something goes wrong, so we need to stand our ground and be strong with others around us. Believe me, I know this can be hard.

It was not an easy life, taking care of my ex-husband. I was his wife, his confidant, his nurse, his therapist, and anything else he needed me to be. I did not complain and did what I had to do to look after those I loved. But, having someone in your household that is unbalanced is difficult for everyone involved and usually, it is the caregiver that must deal with it all. My ex-husband would have good days and bad days and days where I would wonder why I had not gone insane myself.

For the most part, it was our child and me. His dad was just another person living in our house. My ex-husband did spend time with our child in the beginning, but gradually he lost interest, engulfed in his own emotions. He spent many hours sleeping or in bed with migraines. The curtains would be drawn closed and the room dark. There were many times we had to be quiet when he was feeling his emotional ups and downs. Even bouncing a balloon between my child and I would bother my ex-husband. So, we would leave the house to play outside to give him the peace he needed. It was not easy to keep a happy face on at times, especially for the sake of our child. The emotions would play at my heartstrings, sad that this child was growing up without their father doing the fun things fathers do with their kids. And yet, these are situations you have to get over, deal with or make a decision on how you wish to live your life and everyone around you.

After years of trying to deal with my ex-husband's turmoil of emotions and helping him get through life, things changed drastically when he called me from work one day, asking me to pick him up. He had gone from job to job, trying to hold things together and he tried. Oh, he tried, but his mental state was deteriorating as the years passed. He could not do it anymore. He had left work on his lunch break and called me. He was not sure where he was, but he told me that if I just drove toward the address of a new job that he had just started only three days before, I should find him walking on the sidewalk.

I had been driving him back and forth to work as of late after he had been in a few accidents and had a few other questionable incidents. One time he had almost crashed into the car in front of us, which had one of my siblings and their young family in the car. Had I not yelled at him to stop, that incident could have ended badly for both our families. My parents who were not with us at the time, would have been dealing with the outcome of that crash, which involved all their children and grandchildren.

We must have had angels with us that day because the car stopped on a dime, with the back end lifting slightly. Thank goodness it didn't topple over. It was as if some force had stood in front of the car, much as you see superheroes do in movies or comic books. As time passed, he began to run through a few red lights, something he would not dare to do before. And he had disregarded other rules of the road with our young child and me in the car. I knew it was time to take the keys away from him before he hurt himself or someone else. He was just not able to think straight anymore.

That day he called on me to pick him up, had been an emotional day for him. He had been overwhelmed by the chaos in the lunchroom at work and could not handle the emotions swelling up inside of him. So, he had left not wanting to return. I could hear the fear, the panic in his voice when he had called. The feeling that everyone was watching him, judging him, or out to get him was real for my ex-husband. I wondered if he had not taken his medications again, or if his body had become immune to them. Which meant his emotions were not being kept in check. Either way, the past few months had seen his mental health deteriorate and he had just hit a breaking point. I feared this time, it was going to be a long journey back for him to find any kind of normalcy in his life. We had been back and forth to doctors more than usual, but it seemed we still had not found the right remedy to aid in balancing his emotions.

Frantic to give my ex-husband the right care, I quickly called his new psychiatrist. He was a man we had been sent to after I had continued to search for someone to help him with whatever he was experiencing. I felt like we were working with a broken bureaucratic system that was not helping my ex-husband at all. It was just a repeat of going to the hospital, talking to him, and then they would send him home. Fast forward to today, it seems things have not changed much when it comes to helping someone out with mental illness.

I had hoped that by calling the doctor, he would be able to suggest another hospital to take my ex-husband to since he was the expert and would know how to best navigate the hospital system. I felt the one we had been going to was either too busy to attend to my ex-husband's needs, or not taking his emotional decline seriously and the time for just talking and sending him home, I felt was over. He was losing touch with reality

The psychiatrist suggested another hospital and I raced out the door, my heart pumping hard. I could feel my temples pulsating and the adrenaline rushing through my body. I had tears in my eyes, wondering what shape I would find my ex-husband in this time. But I also had some hope that maybe with the doctor helping us along and a different hospital to take my ex-husband to, maybe, this time would be different. Maybe this hospital would evaluate him and suggest a program to monitor my ex-husband and make sure he stayed on track so that he could function through life, better than how he was.

When we have other ailments, we have regular checkups with the doctors or get sent to a specialist. That, in turn, may set us up for regular appointments so that the ailments continue to be monitored. With my ex-husband, then, and with others, I have heard in recent months, does not seem to be the case. The patient is checked, given some medications, and sent on their way. Meanwhile, their health continues to deteriorate, and nobody is checking up on them to even notice.

There were many times, my ex-husband would have an emotional breakdown and knew he needed someone to talk to. Yet when he would finally go to the hospital, he would be told the psychiatrists on staff did not have an appointment available. If he were lucky, someone would come out and quickly talk to him, then make an appointment for months later. Other times, we would be sent home with an appointment for a doctor that had a waiting list longer than Santa's Christmas list.

When he would finally get in to see the psychiatrist, his episodes would have subsided, and my ex-husband would not remember what had upset him so much to go to the hospital in the first place. Without discussing his issues, the psychiatrists were never really able to get down to the root of his problems, nor was I able to attend the appointments to help either. So, it became this never-ending journey of my ex-husband going to the hospital, maybe, having someone quickly talk to him, or just be given an appointment for months later, and sent home. No wonder his emotional state continued to decline when we were not able to see where he was headed.

We would go home, and I would be the one on the receiving end that had to deal with what my ex-husband was going through. I had no training in mental health. I could only provide love and knowing my ex-husband, could calm him down enough to make him be at peace with himself for a short while. But of course, other episodes would disrupt his days. With each episode, even though he took medication to calm him down, he would have more difficulties coping with everyday life.

There had been many hospital visits in the past, given my ex-husband's mental state of mind, but I knew this particular day was going to be different. My ex-husband had not sounded good on the phone when he had called me. He was scared and confused. Paranoid really. And I had seen the way he was deteriorating through the months. He would usually bounce back, and things would slowly return to what we called normal. I was sure the day had come, however, that to keep our young child and myself safe, we had to leave and begin a new life.

This was difficult to do because there was still love in my heart for the man. There were many tears shed throughout the marriage as I tried to figure out how to help him and provide a safe feeling environment for our child and his other children. I knew there were going to be many more tears after we left, because not only was I worried about his welfare, but I also was going to have to raise our child on my own and with no financial help either.

The knowledge that our child was going to grow up not having a normal relationship with his father and not being able to see him the way one would in a family environment, pained my heart every day. I also did not want my child's wonderful relationship with their half-siblings to change and I hoped they would stay in our lives. They were good kids, but I knew things can never stay the same.

I knew it was time to make a change. I had tried over the years to get my ex-husband help for his ailments, with no progress, given as I said what I feel is a broken system through government help, hospitals, and the like. He was tired of going to see doctors. There was nothing much they could do for him and would just spend his days in solitude. Most days he would pack his knapsack, take his bike to the library, and be gone all day.

Where once there was a man full of love, now there was this empty shell of a man that had a hard time coping with even the simple, everyday things in life. His mental instability had changed him, and I had exhausted all the avenues to help him become more stable. He understood he was a danger to us, so he had decided to move in with another family member that maybe would be better equipped to help him.

We spoke every day, for a long time, and shortly after my ex-husband had moved, he had asked me to call his new doctor. He felt he still was not concentrating well and wanted me to provide the doctor with my ex-husband's past situation. Of course, I would do anything to get him on a path to recover, and it would give me a chance to ask the office if they had been able to get the file from the previous doctor. In that way, I hoped that they would have a better picture of what my ex-husband had been going through all these years.

I did not think they would speak to me, since we were newly separated, but for my ex-husband's sake, I thought I would try. I remember calling the office hoping to have the doctor call me back since they were several hours out of town and as soon as the receptionist found out who I was, her mannerisms towards me changed. She bluntly assured me the doctor would not be calling me back. I tried to explain that my ex-husband had asked me to call, but I knew my words were falling on deaf ears. The woman said a few rude words and hung up.

My ex-husband was on his own and I feared his situation would only get worse without someone monitoring him closely. But my hands were tied to help him. On the one hand, I had been relieved my ex-husband had moved in with a family member since he would not be alone, but I also was concerned his ailments would not be monitored as I had done for so many years. Sure enough, he had experienced a relapse several years later and almost lost his life.

Is it any wonder that I began to develop health issues given the stress I was under? But like a true caregiver, I put my issues aside to make sure everyone else was looked after. Through the many years prior, I had kept my ex-husband's secret of his emotional instability to myself at his request, telling no one, not even family or friends. It was a crazy time trying to deal with this all alone and in silence.

Even if I wanted to find outside help, with psychologists, physiatrists, or other experts, I had no time to see them, given everything I was juggling in our lives. I tried my best to live as normal a life as I could. But I had only been denying what I knew to be true. My ex-husband was not mentally stable, and he needed more help than stronger pills, different pills, or other stuff prescribed for him, which in some instances, made him more suicidal, instead of helping to keep him emotionally balanced.

With everything my ex-husband was going through, I thought he did well to deal with life as he had. But when he called me that day in a panic, I feared for what he would do to himself, to us, or others. That day did indeed, mark the changing of all our lives and a new chapter would begin for us.

I continued driving that day until I caught sight of my ex-husband walking in the direction that would eventually take him home and realized he had already walked a good distance. I honked to get his attention and immediately saw the relief on his face. Parking the car on the side of the road he jumped in. He was an emotional wreck. I tried to calm him down and told him we had to go to the hospital where they could help him. He agreed and as we drove, I heard him talking to himself and the things he said. I had this fear that he would yank on the steering wheel and kill us both.

When we finally got to the hospital, the woman at the front desk was not moved at all by my explanation of what had brought us to the Emergency Department that day. She told us to either visit our family doctor or be added to a waitlist until a psychiatrist could call us back, which would take months. Since I had known my ex-husband, I had never seen his emotions get so out of hand that he would hear voices and I knew this was a lot more serious than some of his other roller coaster days. I felt he needed medical attention to maybe calm him down and I did not think talking alone was going to do it this time. I realized; this hospital was no different than the one closer to our home and all I kept thinking of was, here we go again.

I could not believe that this woman was sending us away. Then again, I should not have been surprised, since it had not been the first time, we had been turned away so nonchalantly. Had our medical system become so overwhelmed that they could not help a person suffering from an emotional explosion? Were there not enough doctors on staff that could handle the type of crisis my ex-husband was experiencing? Or was a mental breakdown not important or understood enough to help someone immediately, given the condition my ex-husband was in? Looking at the woman who was ready to go to the next patient in line, I pointed to my ex-husband who rocked back and forth pleading with the voices in his head to stop telling him to do unspeakable things.

"Soooo", I said as I tried to stay calm, looking at the lady straight in the eyes, "What you are telling me is that I have to take my husband home while he hears voices in his head telling him to hurt us, something he has never experienced before, and pray he does not follow through with what he's thinking? He is psychotic and needs help now."

I know the woman did not like me at that moment, but I did not care. There are times we have to advocate for our loved ones, and this was one of them. The woman huffed and puffed, rolling her eyes at me, and put us both in a room with a very heavy, thick door. My ex-husband was rocking back and forth, still fighting the voices in his head hours later. I felt like I was in a movie, but this was real life. In movies, the ending does not matter, because well, it is just a movie. But in real life, the ending could be devastating, and I did not know how this one would end.

Would he pick up one of the chairs in the room and hit me with it, not realizing what he was doing? Would he kill me right there in the room? I am sure no one would hear me if I screamed given the thick door. It was frightening being in there with him and I wanted to leave for my own safety, but I was too afraid to make any sudden moves as I sat in my chair across from my ex-husband and tried to talk to him and calm his fears. As frightened as I was at that moment, to be in the same room with him, I also did not want to leave him alone, for fear of what he might do to himself.

The hospital did not look busy when we came in, but it took well over two hours or more before someone finally came to see us and where I expected a doctor knowledgeable in handling a mental health crisis such as what my ex-husband was experiencing, it was a social worker that came into the room. I did not know this until my ex-husband informed me the following day. This was a new experience for us, and so I was surprised they did not deal with it differently.

I guess, I did not know fully, how the hospital dealt with cases like my ex-husband’s. But sending a social worker told me my ex-husband's situation was not deemed as the emergency I thought it was. But, when someone hears voices in their head, telling them to do bad things, is that not a situation to attend to sooner rather than later? Before the person has gone crazy and injured others?

When the worker came into the room, they immediately, told me to leave, so that they could speak privately to my ex-husband. Understanding, I stood up to go, but my ex-husband pleaded with them to let me stay, telling them as he sobbed, that I was his wife, his nurse, his strength, his confidant. But they wanted me out, telling me I could be the problem, and barely gave me a chance to calm my ex-husband down before leaving the room.

The entire experience with the nurse at the front desk and the mannerisms of the social worker had left me feeling demoralized. I was beyond exhausted dealing with this all alone and I had hoped this hospital would give my ex-husband the medical attention he may have needed to help him live a better life. Instead, I had to fight to have someone understand that this was not a simple case where you just sent the person home. This was a serious matter. There was no crisis team, that could take me aside either and not only find out what was ailing my ex-husband to be able to help him further but to find out what the situation was at home and maybe calm my own tattered nerves even though you probably could not tell from looking at me at the time.

The staff, the professionals all got to go home at the end of their shifts and did not have to deal with all the emotions of someone suffering from a mental illness, while people like myself, who cared and loved those that could not manage their emotions had to figure out a way to help them deal with them as well as keep the family safe from any possible harm. It is not an easy thing to do sometimes.

I tried to stop the tears that swelled in my eyes and called my parents, to let them know where I was and that I would be late in picking up our child, who was spending the day with them. It took all the strength I had not to tear up again when my child came to the phone to ask where my ex-husband and I were. Something I was not prepared to tell them. They had already experienced their father not coming home a few years earlier after having another health crisis. The other fear that kept running through my mind, was what my ex-husband was telling the person in the room with them. I thought how easily the stories could be turned around, making me look like the bad one.

The hospital kept my ex-husband overnight and he was discharged the following day, arranging for him to attend anger management courses for the next three days. Since I am no doctor, I failed to understand how his mental state would benefit from such a class. His emotions were up and down. Happy, sad, angry, blaming others, paranoid, depressed, suicidal, and so many more emotions that could be felt all in the same day, if not within hours of each other.

Wasn't there a chemical imbalance in his brain? At least that was what we were told in the past. That was why the doctors were prescribing the medications that they were. So how were three days of classes going to help him stop the voices in his head, if his system was out of wack? Forgive me for saying, but I'm sure if classes were the answer to his problem, they would have been suggested a long time ago. But again, I am no doctor and I guess, did not understand the hospital's methodology.

I felt like the event had just been a bandage to calm my ex-husband down for the time being. But what about helping him for the long term? I could not even call the hospital to discuss the situation in hopes that they would re-evaluate my ex-husband's symptoms and bring him back to the hospital to help him further. I knew they would not speak to me given the privacy laws prohibiting them from doing so. I had called my ex-husband's psychiatrist back and he had also informed me not to bother with the hospital as they had already discharged my ex-husband, so there would not be anything I could do at this point. I would have to wait to get him further help the next time he would lose his mind. So, all I had to do was pray that he would not.

My ex-husband's appointment with this psychiatrist was not for some time so we were not even able to turn to him for further help. We were back to handling this crisis alone. The next day when I saw my ex-husband, he told me the voices had subsided, and that the hospital had given him some medication, then sent him home in the morning. He kept assuring me everything was going to be fine. But I knew it would not be.

I was angry that the hospital would not look further into my ex-husband's condition and give more support. I was also sad, that the hospital would not hear me out and take note of his journey; his ups and downs, mood changes, triggers of those moods, anything that could help answer some questions on any further steps to take that would help my ex-husband become more stable. Maybe all he needed was the correct balance of medication to stabilize him or be on a program that would adapt what medications he took to his changing needs. I understood it would not be so cut and dry, but at least with some support, my ex-husband may have been on a better path than the one he had to take.

I was also angry that the psychiatrists my ex-husband had been seeing as of late, probably had an idea that he was getting bad thoughts, yet no one mentioned to me to maybe leave and protect my family or tell me to watch our back. And even if they did not know, nobody at the hospital where I had taken my ex-husband that last time, said anything to me about watching out for my family and myself.

They may not have felt it was a priority, and yes, privacy laws would stop them from discussing any personal issues, but they had not lived the experience nor seen my ex-husband when he would have his emotional declines. I still had a young child to protect, and I felt our needs were not being looked at, considering we all lived in the same house. I'm sure there was a workaround where they could warn me somehow. If anything, I thought it would have been the social worker that would discuss things with me further, but that was not the case.

The laws did protect my ex-husband's personal information, which by the way I knew about it at that time, yes, but at the same time, there was a possible situation that could have arisen from the way my ex-husband was declining, and all that was done for him was to talk to a psychiatrist and send him home. Again, maybe this was all that could be done at the time to keep someone stable, but I was sure there was more help for him, we just had not found it.

After leaving the hospital alone that day, I had gone home to pack a few things for my child and myself. I knew we could not stay in the same house with my ex-husband. Not in the state he was in. I wanted my child to have a future and I wanted to be in that future. So, I stayed with my parents, coming back to check in on my ex-husband the next day, and every day until he had moved in with his family member.

The fear of walking into that house not knowing what my ex-husband would do was real. I put my key in the lock and could feel my stomach turning, wondering what I would find on the other side of that door. I did not know if he was home or not. Everything was dark and quiet. You could hear every sound the house was making. Think of how you feel when you watch a scary movie. You are eating your popcorn and sitting on the edge of your seat. The haunting music is playing in the background. The camera shows a dark shadow hiding behind a door, holding something sharp and ready to strike. The innocent victim walks into their path. Then bam! The unthinkable happens and there are one or two fewer people in the world. And now you have a crime scene.

I feared every day that I would either find my ex-husband hanging from the ceiling or that he would jump out at me and hurt me. My thoughts would run to my child, who I did not want to leave alone. But at the same time, I wanted to make sure my ex-husband was safe. So, what do you do? Do you leave your loved ones to fend for themselves? Maybe some would. Some of us move forward into the unknown at times and hope we come back out in one piece.

When I think of everything that happened then, I wonder how I made it through with my brain intact. For the most part, I am a very positive person and I think that positivity and knowing that this was something I had no choice, but to deal with and had to come out strong, was just something I had to do. I had a kid to raise, and I could not let my mental sanity get the best of me. I had to find a new home for my child and me to move in too, and make sure that my ex-husband was taken care of as well. At the time, he had not decided to move in with his family member, so I was busy looking for a suitable place for him too. That would mean two moves and splitting up our lives, our belongings, and all that goes with a loving family. A picture of a broken heart comes to mind right now.

All the love, the memories, and happiness that once was came to an end. The realization that I would not be growing old with this man, nor possibly reach that amazing, twenty-five or fifty years of marriage to someone I cared for, and my child not having their father around was a hard pill to swallow. And yes, even though, my ex-husband was the one taking pills to help him deal with his mental instability, to no avail, the imaginary pills I had to take to stay sane, had to help do just that. Keep me going until the next event.

I tried to find affordable apartments for my ex-husband that were far enough away, to keep us safe and at a distance from him, but close enough for me to still watch him from afar. But every time I would find a place, my ex-husband would tell me he wanted to put in an application in the same building. This would not keep my kid and me safe, so I eventually ended up staying at my parents' home, where I knew, my ex-husband would not dare to come.

Bless my parents for helping me through this time. My ex-husband eventually chose to move in with his family member who was stronger than me and better equipped to handle his ways. I had approached Social Services to help us out given our financial situation at the time and worried that my ex-husband would end up in a place that would depress him further, so I was relieved when his relative suggested having my ex-husband move in. All in all, it was a good union since both could help each other in different ways.

The following day after I left my ex-husband, I found myself at the courthouse, knowing I had to get custody of our child to make sure he would be safe from his father and not be picked up from school or as he played with friends. That was a difficult thing to do mentally, and the process was not easy either. There were many trips to the courthouse, to make sure I filled out the right papers. It was all so daunting. I did not have the money to go through a lawyer, so I had to do everything myself. Did I do the divorce at the same time? No, in my case, the lawyer had suggested I settle the childcare first. Did I have all the papers that I needed from my ex-husband's doctors to show his instability and that he was a danger to our child if he had custody? I sure did.

When you are dealing with mental health, you don't know what the best decision is to make when it comes to staying or leaving the situation. I had stayed in the marriage, knowing I should have left long ago, but I needed the right proof that my ex-husband would be unstable enough to care for himself, let alone a young child. After dropping my ex-husband off at the hospital that one day, I had the proof I needed and I received custody of our child, making sure he still saw his father as often as he wanted to, but in a public place to stay safer. I never received any child support until years later when my ex-husband came into some money, and even that was not much and not for long. I struggled, but I survived.

I waited for years to get my divorce, afraid if my ex-husband would harm himself or us. A pang of guilt I would not be able to live with. If it were not for him giving my name so freely, to his creditors to collect on his newly acquired debts, I probably would not have gone through with it for many years after. My fear was so great. But one I had to get over and move on, leaving the past behind.

We visited with my ex-husband once a month, as I said, always in a public place which usually was a mall. Fear that my ex-husband would push us down the stairs if we ventured to the lower part of the mall, I would let him go down the stairs first, holding our child behind me. I would hold on to the railing with my other hand for dear life. My fear stemmed from something that my ex-husband had written in a book that I saw open on the kitchen table the day before I picked him up and took him to the hospital. It contained a lot of frightening things he wanted to do to people, including us. I did not know how to approach this situation once I had seen what he had written. I was afraid to talk about it with my ex-husband in case, he would lash out at me or our child since I now knew his secret. But I knew I had to discuss it with someone. I never got the chance, given my ex-husband's emotional breakdown the following day.

There were so many more events that took a toll on my health, and how I coped with these events to come out strong, so I am putting together another book called, Bipolar Love, Experiencing Mental Illness From The Other Side, because I want to share my experiences, in whatever form that will materialize, in hopes that my stories will help others deal with similar situations.

Also, a reminder that you are not alone. Caregivers go through emotional turmoil as well and we do not count the many times we, ourselves hit rock bottom as we look after others. So, if you are reading this and are a caregiver just remember to stop and look after yourselves too. Before you get too sick to know you should stop and change things. If it means getting others involved to help you through the difficult days, then do it. If you have to get outside help or change things to keep everyone's sanity, take a close look at what is best and move forward with some new steps. Too often we just keep on going and become ill in the process.

Or if you know a caregiver who is giving it their all, help them along as best you can, either through your assistance or guiding them towards someone else that can give a helping hand. Just do not let them work themselves to the bone without giving attention to their bodies and their mental health that they need to keep living their healthy life. Because remember, that they may be so involved with going through the motions every day as they care for a loved one that they do not even realize what is happening to them.

My caregiving days did not end when I moved away from my ex-husband. As I mentioned, I moved in temporarily, with my parents, expecting to move into my own place in the coming weeks, but my father wanted me to stay so that we could all help each other. I could not refuse the opportunity to raise my child in a decent, safe home with family.

After splitting up our furniture and belongings with my ex-husband, I moved the rest of our things into the basement of my parent's home. It was crowded with their furniture down there also, but we made it work. There, we began our new life. Our bedrooms were on the top floor with everyone else, but the rest of our living area surrounded the basement and of course, we had the run of the entire house, if we wanted.

As grateful as I am that we were able to stay there, and as much as I love my parents, it was difficult to move back with them. Their rules were very old-fashioned, very traditionally European and I was not; having been raised all my life in Canada. I remember once going to visit an old family friend and returning home around 9 pm. That was too late for me to be out according to my father.

My kid and I quietly walked into the dark house, thinking my parents had gone to bed early. As soon as we walked in, we heard my father's angry voice. It startled my kid and me. My father stood at the top of the stairs, much like he had when we were younger, blasting me for staying out so late and keeping my young child out, with no husband to protect me. Little did my father know that I had never had that protection. I had always been an independent woman, so it took a lot of patience, and a lot of letting many little things go, to keep the peace. Believe me, it was not easy, especially, having to protect my child from what I thought to be old barbaric ways, which they were not used to, not to mention the family squabbles.

So, there again, began other stresses, for us both, and they would eat at me through the time we were there and having to live under my parents' rules. Had I believed more in myself, had I been stronger to do it on my own, I would have not only set some boundaries but probably left. Only, I doubted my ability to find a decent place for me and my child. Plus, it now seemed to be a given, that I was the best one to look after my parents and I knew they could use the help as they got older. Again, I was trying to look after everyone else but me and my offspring. It would be years before I did finally find the strength to take a stand and do what I knew was the best choice for me to make and keep my sanity.

About two years after moving in with my parents, one of them had a heart attack. Thankfully, it was not a major one. They had surgery and began to heal. A few years after that, my other parent suffered a mild stroke. It took many months for them to bounce somewhat back. I helped as much as I could, and even my child would help wherever possible. Think the health scares for our family was done? Nope. I then ended up having a major surgery, where I am grateful, I can still walk with my own beautiful legs and swing my arms about. A few years after that, my parent that had the first stroke had a second one. This one was very bad. We are fortunate that they are still with us, although in a different capacity.

My mental sanity was already stretched from caring for my ex-husband, my parents' earlier health scares, and my health. Now, aside from trying to raise my kid, I had to care for my ill parent and as I mentioned, my physical health was not good. I had been in a car accident years before, and the doctors thought that accident, severed my spine which was causing me difficulty in walking, using my hands, and other issues. Things were only getting worse, and it had to be stopped. Emergency surgery was my best choice. So here I was, the one that was supposed to look after everyone else, but now I needed tending to. It took a while, but I got back to a new normal and healed better than I thought I would to which I credit all the years of working out and eating well towards my healing. Not to mention my wonderful energy healers, and there were several. I know with the work each one of them did on me helped to make me stronger and stronger.

It took me a few months before I could drive and let me tell you the pain, I would feel in just checking a simple blind spot was tremendous. My hands would grip the steering wheel and stay bent in that position. I would have to slowly wait for my hands to come back to a point where I could unbend them. And I could no longer multitask the way I once could. It was hard to have my kid watch me in this weakened state. I was always the strong one. Nothing got me down.

But I knew I had to smile through it all, even with my constant pain which became chronic. I had to keep going because if I stopped and became upset or sadden by my disposition, I would give up. I certainly was not prepared to do that and spend my life feeling miserable. My kid deserved better than to watch me deteriorate through the years. I deserved better than that.

These challenges such as being a caregiver which is tough enough, and then becoming ill ourselves, can do one of two things. It can break us, making us weaker and we give in to the illness, becoming its victim. We can begin to feel sorry for ourselves, maybe become depressed, and tired of the ailments. We may stop enjoying life because we are so busy feeling all our aches and pains. And of course, we are not much help to our loved ones who are not well either.

Or we break free of the monkey mind that tells us we are ill, and instead thrive, finding new life, new ways of living, and being full of vigor, full of stamina. Maybe feeling better than we have in years. Yes, we may still have our ailments. Yes, we may still have a difficult life caring for others, but we are not letting all of this stop us from still enjoying life. Even if that may be in a different capacity

I was never able to go back to working out the way I used to or moving furniture around in my home like it was light as a feather. If I had a bunch of errands to run, I had them all done in one day. I was Mrs. speedy. No longer was that the case. I had to adapt to a new normal and accept where I was at in life and continue living it with joy and anticipation for what was to come the next day and the next and the next. That is just the journey of life.

I remember shortly after my surgery, my parents were so worried and concerned that I had made my way downstairs to my place, too quickly and ready to resume my life. I had experienced enough days healing in bed. I had to get my mind out of the negative thoughts, sad thoughts of 'the woe is me' syndrome I was feeling. Plus, I no longer wanted to be a burden on my parents, especially with the one who was still not doing well after that first stroke. I had to heal so that I could be of some help.

I still had to be careful of course, and I was not going to push things, but I had to at least begin somewhere to rebuild my strength and willingness to move forward. My kid, who had just started high school, was cooking our meals as I guided them. I was not able to lift much weight still, so every movement was difficult and painful. It is the hardest thing when you cannot even lift a glass without it feeling heavy, let alone not dropping everything in sight, which was what was happening to me.

Still, I would muster the strength to do what I could which was not much those days, but it was a start to progress forward in healing. I am so grateful for the toaster oven we had, which made things easier for my kid to put a meal together and bake things. I thought it was safer than using the stove or the oven. A very old stove, at that. One that my parents had bought back when I was a teenager if not younger.

So, with my limited ability, I had to make my life work differently. It had been a few years after my surgery when my one parent fell so very ill. My other parent was old and ailing but bless them as they were strong, and we shared the duties of looking after my ill parent to the best of our ability. They were going through their own emotional turmoil of watching the love of their life, someone they had been married to for almost sixty years, deteriorate before their eyes. I felt like it was up to me to make sure they both were taken care of. After all, I was the one that lived there.

We had spent many exhausting days at the hospital after my parent had the stroke and we did not know for the first three days if they would make it through the night. My one parent and

I would leave the house very early in the morning and stay at the hospital all day. One of my other siblings would do the night shifts. When we reached home at the end of the night there were often many phone calls of concerned family and friends, wanting to know how my parent was doing, so even though I was exhausted and had not had dinner yet, I would call each one back and speak with them briefly. I was touched by the amount of love we received from each call.

The next day my parent and I would start the day over again, for the next three months. It took a toll on all of us. Once we got my ill parent home, we had to adjust the place to accommodate a wheelchair and the changing health conditions. We had therapists coming to the house, PSW's to help us, and many times they would not even show up, and I would wonder how to help my parent, given the strength I no longer had to move them and help them how I needed to. Somehow, there was always someone coming to help at the right moment.

It was another crazy time with the front door becoming a revolving one of people coming and going. Our sleeping patterns changed since my other parent and I would be up most of the time, tending to my parent's needs. Many times, I would sit on the ground by my ill parent's bed, singing or caressing their hand to soothe their fears. There were nights I tried not to wake the other parent up and getting angry at my inability to do things on my own, given my health, but I would have no choice. I would have to wake them up to help tend to my ill parent. How interesting life was. In the past, I used to work out so much that I could lift a lot of weight. Now, when I needed my strength more than ever, I did not even have the strength to lift my parent's head to fix the pillow. I guess the Universe was telling me to slow down.

I remember how both myself and my other parent would jump the minute we would hear a peep out of my ill parent, not knowing what was happening to them. We were still getting used to the new health changes and there was a lot of emotional upheaval in the family and many different attitudes to deal with. Everybody had an opinion.

Learning a thing or two from looking after my ex-husband, I realized I had to put some simple rules back in place to make sure we all survived the situation we were in without much harm to our health and our sanity. I remember when we first spoke to the government representatives, who encouraged us to put my ill parent in a nursing home, feeling we couldn't manage them at home and returning two years later to find that we had adjusted things and were making it work.

The reality was that given the health issues my ill parent had, they probably would have received better care with nurses and doctors present that could tend to them in a nursing home, however, we did not want to do that, and the decision was made to bring my parent home where they could have the love and care of family. But, given the circumstances, we were in and both our health of myself and my healthier parent, we should have employed a full-time caregiver from the start to help because there was a lot of physical work to do, that I was unable to perform, and it would be difficult for my other parent to do alone. There were other things to consider as well like how to get my ill parent to a doctor or dentist or even just to get a haircut. It meant getting special transportation for wheelchairs. It would be a challenge to move them and if they had another health scare or need an ambulance, we would be at the mercy of the system.

But there was an issue of wanting to save, save, save those dollars at the expense of our health. Sometimes, we must keep our sanity, and saving a few dollars to not get the help needed, especially, in a situation like ours, can make a difference in the caregiver's health and their mental sanity. It is just not worth it. For the first three months, it was just my parent and myself looking after my ill parent.

We did, however, have family come and help with some things and when the PSW's did come, they were ever-changing and not fully aware of the special care needed. So, I made sure I was there when they came to the house.

The stress of caring for someone at home does not stop only at the caregivers. It affects the entire family who loves you as well and has to watch you work away, day and night. Sure they can help here and there, but for the most part, it is the caregivers who take charge and there is generally one main person doing that. In our family, it was me having to make sure things ran smoothly. That went for making sure equipment was charged up and working well, supplies had to stay stocked. Chores, and caring for my ill parent also had to be taken care of. So, my kid who thankfully was older now was able to fend for themselves, which gave me more time to care for my ill parent. Still, I needed to make sure I provided them with the attention they also needed.

They were not without having their stresses over watching me try to get through the days. They knew how challenging it was for me and it took its toll on them too. They were constantly reminding me to not overwork myself, knowing how far I could push forward, and suffer for it later. There were late nights when my kid would find me at the brink of tears at my other parent's bedside, gently trying to wake them, hoping not to frighten them in the process, but I needed their help to tend to my ill parent's needs. They were so exhausted they would not wake at my gentle whispers or nudges. I would be watching their chest, to see if they were still breathing. But I knew things were taking their toll on them too. Again, I was angry at my ill health, which would not allow me to care for my beautiful parent's needs more.

Some of those nights were at three or four in the morning, and my kid would come downstairs asking if they could help me, knowing the work had to be done, but I was not going to drag them into the mix, not to mention it was not something I felt was appropriate for a young person to help with certain things. They did enough through the days when they were home from school to help with other duties and had become a master at using the lift. I was grateful they were there, especially the times when we had to contact emergency services. Once, the ambulance attendants could not figure out how to move my parent onto their stretcher, using our lift. The wheels from my parent's bed did not line up with their stretcher and they were at a loss as to how to move my parent. But my kid took charge and knew exactly what to do and the men were able to safely get my parent on their stretcher and to the hospital.

I wondered how long before my healthier parent would recognize that we needed more help. But they were a workhorse and I felt were not facing reality, thinking we could continue to do it all ourselves. But we were both burning out and there was a lot I could not help with. Had I not made some changes, in the end, I am sure both our health would have continued to suffer and deteriorate as mine was already doing as the months and years passed.

There was a lot of emotional turmoil and new things to adjust to, given the devastating change in my ill parent's life. I thought it interesting how the universe had prepared me to care for both my parents through the experience of looking after my ex-husband years before. I found there was a lot of patience and understanding I needed and so much more inner strength to pull out that I did not know I had. Just goes to show how we build on our lives as we go, always being at the right place. The Universe surely knows what it's doing.

As hard as it was, I found myself having to again leave my parent's home, after caring for my ill parent for a couple of years. Their health continued to deteriorate, and so was mine as I continued to visit doctors, therapies, energy healers, and whatever other modality I thought could help me continue to cope with everything I was going through. I just wanted to stay strong so that I could continue to provide what I could for my ill parent.

Lack of sleep, trying to lift things I should not be didn't help my healing, not to mention the dynamics of family rivalry which was a different stress component. I felt like that frog that was slowly boiling in a pot of water and cooking to its death, instead of realizing what was happing and jumping out. I still had to be careful with my back issues as I could end up in bad shape if I forced myself too much, but there was not anyone else to help us some days, and I struggled to do what I could to the detriment of my health.

Coming out of meditation one day, I had seen a vision of me packing and I knew this was my higher self, God, the Universe, call it what you wish, but something was telling me I needed to stop straining my body, because, as I said before, I was going to need a caregiver soon to help me, and I certainly did not want to go down that road.

Reluctantly, my kid and I moved out and I have been working towards re-healing my body once again. We hired outside caregivers for my parents, and although it was not the way I wanted to see things go, sometimes others make choices for us, and they may be blessings in disguise. Both my parents now have round the clock help and as much as I would have preferred that they have love and care from their kids, at least they are being cared for by others that can have a better handle on things, instead of suffering through what I would not be able to assist with.

As I write these pages now, I wanted to use this space to share some of the things I did that helped me keep things organized and keep myself sane, in either situation. I hope that some of these simple steps can help you navigate your life. Each circumstance is different, and you must find what works for you, but do not lose hope. Remember also, that things are ever-changing, so give yourself time to rest and recuperate from the more tiring and stressful days, and don't be so hard on yourself if you can't get to everything on your list because the days will take their toll on you if you let them.

Instead find the solutions that work for everyone in your family, including yourself. Even if it means having to break many beliefs or old traditions and marking your boundaries for when you say yes or no to something or someone. Sometimes it means standing up to other family members, which can be difficult but lets us come into our power. Do not be afraid to do things differently, because you are the one that is living this life. You are the one that knows best what decisions will work and which ones will not. You also are the one that knows your body, your strength, and how much abuse you want to give yourself before your body breaks down. So, it is a decision of whether you wish to still be around to enjoy your loved ones healthily or sickly. Or worse, not even be here because you have made yourself so ill, caring for everyone else, your health has deteriorated until you expire.

Take your days one at a time and always help each other however you can, but always remember to give yourself the same love you give others. That is if you still want to be around to continue to love those you care so much for. And if you wish to live!

I truly hope my stories will help you not make some of the same mistakes I did and learn from the things that worked or didn't for me. There were a lot of lessons I learned through my journey, and they all taught me something about myself. As well as about others. I learned I was stronger than I thought I was. I learned to speak up and hold my ground. I learned I had so much love to give and received so much back from those I looked after. I also learned who was there for me and who was not.

No matter the outcome, I knew I had played an important part in the lives of my loved ones, and had I not been there, things could have turned out different. So, I am grateful for all the good and the bad, the decisions and indecision I have made because it has brought me to today.

There were many days when I wondered if I had done enough and had made a difference in the lives of those I loved and cared for. There still are some days when I wonder, but then I remember many of the things I did that were important. So, everything I did was enough. I am Enough! Remember, that you too are enough!

Chapter Two

Simple Step Number 1

Getting The Help You Need

I am always saying how you, as a caregiver are important too and if you wish to continue providing the best care for your loved ones, you must keep yourself as healthy and as sane as you can so that you continue looking after those you love without other ailments popping up on you.

When I fell in love with my ex-husband, I thought love would see us through the difficult times, but I soon realized that dealing with someone who suffered from a mental illness was not something I was equipped to handle. At the time I did not know fully, what was going on with him. He would burst out in angry fits or get emotional and unable to cope with situations or just life in general. Sad, happy, depressed, and wanting to stay in solitude. He did not really understand what was going on with his emotions either. I knew something was not right, but I was no doctor. Just a simple woman wanting to make sure my ex-husband did not lose himself in whatever emotional turmoil he was experiencing.

As I mentioned previously, we did not discuss his situation with family or anyone else, given the stigmas that still surround mental illness today. So, I dealt with his emotional rollercoasters on my own. There were times he felt suicidal and times he was on such a high that I knew it was just a matter of time before he came crashing down hard. We would ultimately end up at the hospital emergency ward, hoping they could help ease his fears. Maybe if I had been a little more insistent with my ex-husband to discuss his situation more in-depth with doctors given his emotional outbursts, there may have been someone out there that understood what was ailing him or knew a person, that knew another person that could direct us towards further help for my ex-husband.

I didn't realize at the time, that the pressures of keeping everything to myself and handling all that I was, were slowly weighing on me. Even though I was young and strong. Remember that stress can play an important role in our health and if we take on more than what our brains, our bodies can handle, we will shut down. Either in the form of a nervous breakdown or other illness, so it's important to pay attention to what is going on as you handle the situations facing you.

Are you getting overworked, stressed, or upset at what is going on around you? Do you feel guilty or angry at someone for the things they did or didn't do? Are you allowing yourself to get pulled into or manipulated into a situation that could have been avoided? Maybe you got screamed at and thought it was better to just do the deed and be done with it. Are you confused or embarrassed by your loved one's actions towards you or even to others?

Ask yourself some questions about what feels right or wrong for you and your level of comfortability with the life you are living. Of course, every situation is going to be different. Some people will need more guidance, but others may understand that some actions are not going to be tolerated. But the one question you may need to ask yourself is if your loved one needs a professional to speak to, given their mental disposition. One they may not even be aware they have. Or one you may not fully understand at what depth either. So, if you find your loved one acting strange, don't discard it. Have your doctor diagnose them to find out if they truly do have something going on that is a lot more than just having a different personality.

The other question is to yourself. If you are handling more than what you can comfortably take on, is it time to call in someone else to help you with your loved one, or someone to help you cope with the mental challenges of being a caregiver? Sometimes trying to find the right kind of help can be a daunting task. You may ask why, because as long as you get yourself or your loved ones to a doctor, they can help you. But doctors specialize in various fields so you have to find the right one that can understand the situations you are all experiencing.

The family doctor is always a good start because they can at least direct you further. Given the experience we had with my ex-husband, I would suggest trying to stick to the same doctor if possible since they have an idea of your medical history. They know you best. They also have or at least should have as full a medical record on you as possible. Remember to transfer your files from one doctor to the next so that the new doctor can read up on what is going on. And if you absolutely do not feel comfortable with that doctor, find another one if you can.

My ex-husband and I moved every two years, without fail, so because of the distance from our last doctor, we had to find another one each time. They never got the chance to know us well, because, within two years, we were up and moving again. For this reason, it made things difficult to really get a handle on what was ailing my ex-husband and what his mental state was. Plus, he took pride in making sure he fooled the doctors every time. They saw a well-dressed, athletic person who spoke intelligently, so as far as they were concerned, there was no problem with this man's mental ability to function. I mean, how can you assess someone's mental capacity during a quick appointment unless they were exhibiting very strange behaviors at the time?

It would be years before my ex-husband was diagnosed as having Bipolar. An ailment that eventually took over his mind from a man that could function relatively well in society to one that just wanted to be alone and whose personality changed drastically. It saddened me when his symptoms become so severe that my young child and I had to leave the house, just to stay safe. And frightened me as to what would become of him after he had decided to move in with another family member that was better equipped to handle him. He knew he could hurt us and was afraid if he stayed.

When we moved doctors, I always made sure to have the previous medical records sent to the new doctors, but we were still new patients, that they had to get to know. There were many times my ex-husband would visit the doctor with his changing moods, have his medications altered slightly, or be prescribed something that had been given to him in the past that had no success, and so of course, would not help him now either.

The doctors would talk to him and then, send him on his way home. It was always the same thing. I would discuss my ex-husband's situation in hopes the doctors would understand the severity of his emotional decline as the years passed. The fact that he was constantly at the doctor's office or the emergency department, having to be assisted with his emotional needs, somehow was missed.

I had hoped at some point, one of my ex-husband's doctors would realize something deeper was going on. Thereby, arranging an appointment with a psychiatrist to see where my ex-husband's mental status was at. At least, then he would have a specialist in the field monitoring him and adapting his medications according to his symptoms. Something my ex-husband would have benefited from immensely, given where he was at in his journey of mental health.

These visits would be covered by our health care system, but as we came to understand that the list of people needing to see such a professional was long. And the number of doctors available was short. Leaving us to handle whatever situations arose on our own. The only problem with that was that the deeper mental health issues that could not be dealt with at home, would leave us as the caregivers, racking our brains wondering what to do next to help those we love. And our loved ones, getting worse and worse as time passed, unable to get the necessary medical help or guidance they could benefit from. Which, in turn, would stop all of us really, from living fuller lives. Not to mention our loved ones going in and out of the emergency wards, still trying to figure out what was wrong with them years later.

I guess in my ex-husband's situation, doctors may have thought he was stable enough to not need such an appointment. But I felt that if they understood more of what was troubling him, they would have been able to help him more and I'm sure, he would have had a healthier, more satisfying life today, instead of suffering from his mental disposition.

It's a little frightening to think that there are so many people in the world, never mind just in our country that are suffering from a mental illness, and the last few years have not helped things in that department. Except for the people that have woken up and realized they were in a situation they needed to get out of and took those steps. That could be something as simple as changing jobs to find peace of mind, maybe taking on fewer hours to help deal with loved ones at home or leaving a difficult or dangerous situation altogether.

These past few years have only seen mental illness on the rise for young and old and things don't seem to be getting better. There really is no specialized group that comes in and works with someone with a mental situation. It's usually, just calling our law enforcement if things get out of hand, and they are not trained in the finer arts of dealing with someone with mental illness. Plus, so many families live together, just to be able to afford a decent roof over their heads. So, things can get crowded and tempers may flair easier as people deal with more stress and juggle so much.

Because I was the one monitoring my ex-husband and his moods, I had to keep an eye on any changes I would see in him. It could be in his behavior or feeling on a real high or low.

Sometimes it could be the slightest of mood changes and slowly, every day, I could see the difference in how he acted and the things he said and did. These could be indications of medications that were not working as well as they should have been for him. Or maybe something else was happening. His body could become immune to the medications and of course, if they were not working, he would be back to his high or low moods. We found out years later that some medications should not be stopped without being weaned off them as they could make one suicidal, which were experiences my ex-husband often had. So, keep an eye on your loved ones and watch for subtle changes, and don't hesitate to look for help if you find yourself wondering what is going on.

There were days I knew my ex-husband could benefit from talking to a specialist in the field but, if he did not want to go to the hospital, or the doctor, I could not force him, and I would be left with working through the next difficult periods of his emotional rollercoasters.

We needed to find the right team of doctors that could not only find out what was going on with my ex-husband but be able to continue to work with him and get him back on track. Our family doctors were great, but they were not specialized in the knowledge of Bipolar and thus were not able to help him further. At this time, we still did not know he suffered from this disposition, so not much was done to keep his emotions in check. But again, had I been more vocal with the doctors about what was going on at home, maybe someone would have listened and taken on my ex-husband's case.

There were days when I could see my ex-husband was on a high and I knew it was only a matter of time before he would come crashing down. Those days when he would ask me to hide his medications because he would feel suicidal, were scary, and we would be back to the doctor's office trying to figure out what was going on. There was nothing they could do they would tell us. They would again adjust his medication to the best of their knowledge and send us back home.

Privacy laws had changed in Canada, and it became more difficult for me as the wife, to give my feedback on the emotions I saw from my ex-husband. When we would end up at the emergency department during many of his emotional declines, the doctors would discount the severity of what was going on with my ex-husband and just send him on his way. I think that may have been partly because of my ex-husband not discussing his full emotions with the doctors. Then again, maybe there just was not much they knew what to do for him, given that they were not his regular doctor.

But they never saw the holes in the walls where my ex-husband took out his anger or the words, he would say to me that would wound me or the family of young kids. Words or reactions he would not usually say, given his natural loving nature. The doctors were not the ones who would bundle up a newborn baby and spend hours at the hospital with my ex-husband, wondering how they can help him this time or if I would get him back and acting normal for at least a while. And years later when my ex-husband became dangerous to be around, none of the doctors informed me to maybe pack a bag and move away for a while so that my child and I would be safe. Nobody told me my ex-husband was having thoughts of wanting to harm us. We could have been a statistic, and nobody said anything to us.

I wondered where our rights were. Like the right to know the full extent of the mentality of who we were living with and the right to want to live in a safe environment. If something were to happen, there would not be anyone at the door, ready to help us escape a bad situation. Or anyone to help us deal with any trauma we would experience. That stays with you forever. Had I not had a family to stay with the day we did have to leave the house, I would have been on the streets or in a shelter with my young kid. Yet I had a home I could not stay in because the man I loved, the man who was usually caring and thoughtful was there and wanted to harm us due to his mental instability to control himself. And had I not seen what he had written in that open book, I probably would have still stayed to help, thinking this was just another day as before. Instead, my ex-husband's mind was deteriorating by the day.

I continued to try and find the right doctor for him and finally called my helplines at work. I was sent to a psychologist and told him my story of my ex-husband. It took most of the session for the man to believe I had not come there for myself. He wanted to see my ex-husband and I was grateful he agreed to talk to the psychologist. After several written tests, the man determined that my ex-husband may suffer from Bipolar and sent us to a specialist who knew more about it. I am so grateful for that psychologist because nobody else had taken the time to really, figure out what was going on with him and was able to steer us in the right direction.

We were able to put my ex-husband on medication that helped him to concentrate better. Unfortunately, by the time changes to his medications were made, my ex-husband's mental disposition had already deteriorated to the point where he still was not safe to be around. Had I found these doctors sooner in my ex-husband's journey, I am sure they could have helped him a long time ago. But at least we had a name for what was going on with him and could have the correct medication prescribed moving forward. At the time, I didn't know about energy healing, but I'm sure they too could have helped in some way.

Once we knew what we were dealing with, we were able to then go to the family doctor from time to time to follow up on changing medications. At least the family doctor had a better handle on what to prescribe my ex-husband, instead of offering up different medications that would not always work well, as had been the case in the past. And now, we also had the psychiatrist, that my ex-husband could visit and stay on track with things.

For myself, I was able to somehow manage my emotional stress of looking after my ex-husband on my own, but when I think back to that time, I think I would have benefited greatly, not to mention that they also could have helped us both as well as our young child. Had I not been such a patient person as I am, I'm sure things would have been different for my own mental health and I'm sure my marriage would have broken down sooner, not to mention that had I been more of a retaliative person, things could have exploded many times in our household. And who knows how bad things could have become.

The emotional turmoil that goes along with the stresses of caring for someone, whether it is a mental disposition or another caring role, is not easy and runs the caregiver down too. Different emotional stresses go along with the role. If you have the opportunity, find someone that can also help you and the family go through everything you are experiencing, because it throws everyone for a spin. People can get angry with the lack of attention you give to one and the extra you give to another. Time is taken away from giving your love to other family members, including to yourself. Exhaustion sets in and your mind races as you try and figure out what is going on and when will it all end. Where do you go for help? Who can help? Do we expose your secrets to the outside world, and on and on the questions, the concerns, the craziness of it all goes.

There are professionals you can involve and talk things out with and if you check with your local areas where you live, or through government assistance, there may be volunteer groups you can connect with. Here in Ontario, there is an Ontario Caregivers volunteer group you can contact that will have people that can listen to you as you go through difficult times. Check with any health plans you have as they may cover certain therapy visits and don't forget to check with your doctor as depending on what is going on and what they know, they can guide you. Remember it's not just psychiatrists that deal with mental health, but phycologists, and psychotherapists that are available to help too. There are others in your communities that can also lend a helping hand and guide you, like your religious leaders, social workers, or coaches who specialize in specific fields.

There are also many sights on the internet where you can find nearby therapists and other assistance, to help you get through what you are experiencing. Maybe even give you other helpful information. Just as always, be careful who you connect with and the information you give out.

Depending on the sights you find, you can share information with like-minded people who understand what you are going through. Sometimes just knowing others are experiencing the same thing you are is enough to help. When you can share the knowledge you all have, it just makes the load a little easier to bear not to mention that you realize you are not going crazy. That the feelings you are experiencing as you care for those you love are real and if you do not look after them can leave you scarred for the rest of your life.

Speaking with others who have gone through some of the same experiences you are having may also help to give you the information you may not have considered or known about that can assist in healing the entire family. There are different approaches some people take that may help you too. And there certainly is a lot to learn as we uncover more information about mental health.

When it came time to taking care of my ill parent, I was a little older and of course, having more health issues. The mental toll that situation took on me was a lot heavier. Or maybe it was just having to handle both situations in my life. Having a difficult time coping, I had reached out to my family doctor and was told to call my helplines at work. There I could find a psychologist or other professional to help me deal with all the stresses that came with caring for my ill parent and all the family dynamics that were stressing me out more.

Failing that, I would have to find my own psychiatrist to help me cope, which could be costly, since I had no mental diagnosis, and it would not be covered by my government plans. I had walked out of the doctor's office not knowing which way to go. One would only offer me a few sessions and then I would be on my own and the other would be expensive and I could not afford it. Plus, I did not have time to go running around to doctor's offices and leave my healthier parent alone with my ill parent. So, here I was, sacrificing my mental sanity and my health again. I have to say that the one thing that was helpful through the pandemic was that with many things turning to online, connecting to doctors would have been easier since you could contact them from the comfort of your own home.

I knew I just needed someone to talk things out with, maybe to just listen and help me think things out. Plus, I was not sure if a few sessions with a psychologist would do it. There were only a handful of solutions opened to me since I was not suicidal. What concerned me was that even though, thankfully, I was not, I am sure there was some form of stress or depression going on at the time, given what I was going through. I feared that I didn't know how everything was going to affect me in the months, moving forward if I didn't change something. I had reached a difficult point.

I ended up at my Natural Path's office and was given something natural to help calm my tattered nerves. It was something my ex-husband had taken years ago to help him wean himself off the doctor's medications and on to this natural product. It was St. John's Wart. But, before you run out to buy it, you need to check things out with your doctor first. Medications, natural or not are specific to the person's needs and everything else they are taking must be taken into consideration. For my ex-husband's experience, with St. John's Wart? Well, I did indeed get my ex-husband back for a couple of years, while he took that medication, but he also crashed with his emotions after the two years as his body became immune to what he was taking. He eventually, ended back on the medications from the specialists.

Experiencing all I had, I realized it not only was important to find the right doctors who know what is wrong with your loved ones and can prescribe the right medications given the situation, but it is also important to get help for yourself as the caregiver. That help does not end at getting any medications for you to deal with whatever stresses you are feeling as you care for your loved ones, but it also includes finding time for yourself. If you do not sleep right, or eat right, or keep your stress levels down as you deal with all you must juggle, you will put more pressure on yourself and your body and that can only open you up to more disease and like I said, before you know it, you too will end up needing a caregiver. So, take some action before you burn out to the point of not being able to recover.

If you have the time and like to learn, find books to read or some inexpensive courses to help you deal with what you are going through. For example, sometimes when you are caregiving, you may get resistance from other family members who do not agree with the way you are handling things. That alone can add to stress levels. There may be courses you find that help you to understand or deal with difficult people, which in turn enables you to handle various situations, possibly removing some of those stress levels.

Make sure that you are keeping an eye on other family members as well. Caring for loved ones can take a toll on everybody involved as mentioned. Sometimes we get so caught up in helping those who are sick, we forget about the other people around us who also need our love and support. We may forget to handle things that need tending to or continue to put them off. Lack of that all can weigh on other family members. Others may see us getting sicker from all we are doing and try to take us away from the situation, because they see what is going on. But we may not see it so clearly. They can become angry or frustrated with us for giving our life away and not taking care of ourselves.

People may not want to be in the environment any longer, caring for others, or dealing with the family dynamics of having someone who is not well in your home. One can easily slip into bad habits, like starting to drink to forget about the troubles around them or get lost in drugs or other addictions because they are having trouble handling difficult situations. The stress and anxiety everyone is feeling can tear families apart if you are not careful to see the signs.

Sometimes it is necessary to make changes to your home or the way you do things, to accommodate the person not well and that too can cause stress. Do you move into a smaller place or rearrange an area of your home, their home? There can be big costs involved, not to mention renovations you may not want to cope with as you care for someone. There are government help programs that can assist with some of the finances of changing your house to accommodate an ill family member, so you can contact various bodies to help you out.

There may be different generations that may move in together and that too can cause friction, because one is so used to doing things a certain way, only to change and adapt to accommodate everyone. Not to mention that a usually spacious place can become crowded, very quickly.

So, make sure you stay vigilant on everyone's conditions as best you can. Even your own. Because tempers can flare, others' health can become hindered, and it is easy to give up. That by the way, is when you know you should get help and work out a different solution. Be prepared to make some difficult decisions, like having to move your loved one out of your home or their own and making other arrangements for their care. Or for you.

Caregiving is not easy and asks for your physical and mental demands. Especially so when you have been going through life and all has been fine until one day you find yourself in the caregiving role and cannot cope with all that is being asked of you.

So, be ready and adapt to the changes as best you can and find that help you feel you need in whatever areas of your life. Even a little bit of assistance is good. It can be someone helping with chores, like coming in to clean your home instead of you doing it or lending a hand to care for your loved one.

Or it can be finding the right doctors that can help you cope with what you are going through, as well as the right doctors that can assist with your loved one that is not well so that you can help them live the best life they can. Finding the help, you need in all areas of your life, I feel is so very important, because when it comes to caring for someone with a mental illness, or just caregiving in general, can be a long road ahead and you need to keep your strength and sanity intact too.

So, reach out to others and don't go it alone.

Chapter Three

Simple Step Number 2

Healthy Living

We all know when we eat well, we feel more energetic, and our bodies are stronger and healthier. We are also more agile, lighter and it is indeed easier to move about. It is harder for disease to enter our bodies since we are feeding it with the nutrients needed. Eating foods that are good for us, keeps us alive, and helps our moods, our hearts, keeps our bones strong, and helps us remember things.

When I was caring for my ex-husband, there was no time to eat well. There were many trips to the hospital, many after-school events for our young child, and many trips to fast-food places. It was just faster and easier to grab a meal that was already done.

All we had to do was order and pay. But we did not realize how bad those foods were for us and what they were doing to our weight and our health among other things. There is a lot of sugar and salt and other ingredients that are not healthy at all for us when it comes to eating fast foods, canned foods, frozen foods, and boxed foods as well as other foods that carry a lot of these ingredients that our bodies do not like. Not to say they are all bad, but we must look closer at what we are putting in our bodies.

This includes foods that do not agree with us or intolerances we may develop to something we have eaten a million times but is no longer tolerated by the body. It can be allergic reactions, however big or small they may be. We can get a feeling of a foggy brain or sleepy feeling and find it difficult to concentrate. We begin to feel sluggish and overweight. We can feel bloated or develop various marks or rashes on us, which are just one way our bodies try to get us to pay attention to something it no longer wants. Even extra dandruff can be a sign that something is bothering you. Dandruff, that may be eczema. And pimples can go away for some people too, just by cutting out things like dairy products.

The feelings of uneasiness we feel when we do not eat well can continue if we keep eating these foods and our bodies will crave for more if we do not break the cycle. Our energy gets depleted faster, and it makes coping with things harder. We are dealing with enough stress that it is not the best idea to add more to our bodies. Because with everything we are putting ourselves through, our bodies can eventually shut down. Not to mention the many trips to the doctor or medications you may buy to ease your discomfort or ailment.

When I used to cook fresh meals, we all felt better and our skin glowed, but things just naturally changed the busier we got and we did not notice the change until my ex-husband and I began to gain weight. We would buy frozen foods, stop off and pick up fast foods, and eat late. Plus, there were the extra stops with my ex-husband's kids who loved their fast food. We just kept eating what we probably should have stayed away from.

And of course, I loved to cook and bake, especially when his kids would come over, so I would always make something special for them, like cakes and cookies and lasagna and of course pizza which the family all loved. For the most part, I controlled myself, but we all have our weaknesses, and chocolate has always been mine. I remember my ex-husband coming home one night and finding my child and me as giggly and hyper as can be. He suspected I must have made chocolate chip cookies, and one look on the stove and the half-empty pan of cookies told him we had eaten more than our fair share. Everything was funny to us, and we even got my ex-husband laughing most of the night along with us.

It had started with me getting the hiccups and jokingly, I had gone to the fridge and taken a small piece of chocolate, telling my kid, chocolate cures a lot of things. I do not think I was far off because within about five minutes my hiccups were gone. Well, my kid ended up having hiccups shortly after me, which I was certain was from the greasy pizza we had picked up.

Within a few minutes of taking a piece of chocolate, (well we had to test my theory), the hiccups were gone, and we could not believe we had found a remedy for this funny but annoying and sometimes painful involuntary action. Feeling in the mood, my kid wanted to make chocolate chip cookies, and I think we each must have had at least three cookies each, which, yes, we were little piggies that night, because it was not something we would normally do. I do not think we have ever had so many in one night.

Somewhere during those years, I gained about 30 lbs, not watching what I ate or when. I was not taking the time to exercise either, which was something my body was used to doing. I was incredibly stressed and felt horrible but the more I ate foods that were not healthy, the worse I felt. I also could not look at myself in the mirror. I was always a tiny woman and gaining that much weight, especially for a short person like me, at 5 feet and a bit was horrible.

As time passed, I also noticed my ex-husband's food preferences changed. As I tried to get us back to eating better, he instead opted to have more sugary foods, and every morning, not long after breakfast, he would have a soft drink in his hands. He did not drink coffee, but I think he needed the sugar or caffeine intake those drinks provided. I am not saying there is anything wrong with soft drinks, but for him, along with the other food choices he was making, just compounded to extra added weight around his midsection that kept getting bigger. He was also not working out, which didn't make him feel as good as he would when he was more active.

For a man that had several other health issues, he needed to lose the weight, not gain it, but try as I did, I could not get him to change the way his diet had evolved. From a once very trim, athletic person, he ended up a touch overweight and it was not a healthy weight for him. Really, for neither of us, but where I was looking to trim down, he was not caring what he ate. It was almost like he did not care what he did anymore. Although I wondered if it was the change in medication that gave him more sweet cravings. One never knows.

When I moved in with my parents after first leaving my ex-husband, I noticed I had gained a few more pounds after joining them for meals and eating along with them. Even though I brought my own food upstairs, there were still other foods we all shared. There were coffee and Italian cookies in the morning, bread at afternoon and evening meals, potatoes, and sweats that many friends and family would bring since there was always someone stopping by our place for a coffee. Of course, I would bake more since I knew there were sweats other family and friends liked.

There are many foods around that can easily make our mouths water or give us that craving for something and we indulge a little more than we know we should. It is up to us to stay strong and not get pulled into pressure to eat the foods we know we should save for another day. Do you indulge more often than you know you should, and have health issues, or do you enjoy some foods every once in a while, and still stay healthy?

I remember a colleague at work who used to get upset with me when we would go for a break. We both were working on losing weight. I lost it and she did not, yet she would buy donuts and pressure me to have one or more along with her and would push them closer to me when I would politely decline. She had been trying to lose weight for years, and maybe she wanted to take me down with her, but I was not going to get pulled in. In fact, my weight loss inspired her boss who began losing weight, after seeing what I had accomplished. She was eating better and had more energy. I just wish I could have inspired my colleague, but I knew she would lose the weight when she was ready.

For me, I had to take a stand. I had started to cut out many foods just before moving back with my parents and had lost those few pounds. But when I gained it back I knew I had to stop eating with them. So, my kid and I began eating downstairs on our own time and cooking food the way we wanted. Without anyone complaining about how I prepared and cooked our meals differently than the typical European way. I used different and fewer oils and salts, as well as other ingredients which were just enough to flavour our food, the way we liked it. There were no more pressures for us to eat everything on the plate or questions about why we were not eating bread at every meal. The main thing I had cut out of my diet. My small portions frightened my parents and they wondered why I was starving myself, but I had always eaten small portions. It was just not the right type of food before.

The added pressures from my parents not understanding why we were eating on our own eventually subsided, but I had to stay strong and hold my ground, continuing to have our meals on our own so as not to get pulled into eating unhealthy again. I also knew I had to put a stop to the belief that we had to do everything together, just because we lived in the same place. It was vital for me to reach my end goal of eating better.

I had my kitchen and living area downstairs, and I wanted to keep my family unit, separate from that of my parents, making sure my kid had the safe space to grow as close to the way they were used to when we had our home. I did not want to disrupt their way of life more than it had been, given the many changes in our lives already.

We all have our way of doing things, so I did not want to fall into the trap of living the way my parents did and lose my identity as the head of my own family, growing our way, doing the things we wanted to do, and when we wanted to do them.

Sometimes living with other family members can bring about different pressures and there can be difficult bonds to break and live your own life your way, even if it means going against the norms and cultures of others. Some type of separation must occur if you want to keep your sanity. In my case, I had to stay strong to the goals I had set out in my life that were going to keep the weight and junk food down. We were expected to visit others along with my parents, as we had done for many years, but that also meant I would be expected to indulge, having cakes and cookies, and feel more pressured to eat, eat, eat. So, I had to put a stop to this.

I worked towards eating healthier and fought to take back my time whenever I could to exercise and stay in shape so that I could get back to the 'me', I was used to seeing. I immediately felt lighter and much better, once I began to eat right. I also noticed my skin looked better. I would get this flushed feeling throughout the day, (and no it was not a change of life, not yet), where my co-workers would think I had just come back from a brisk walk. But I had not. It was just a feeling that would engulf me and that feeling went away after I began eating better and only returned at times when I would have foods I knew better to stay away from. The foggy brain I would have by eating so much sugar and foods that did not agree with me also went away and I was able to think clearer. I also was not feeling as bloated, and my joints did not ache as much, among other ailments that calmed down. But the minute I would eat more sugars or foods that disagreed with me, the symptoms would come back and I would have another hill to climb.

I was teased and called many names by some family members after losing a lot of my weight and of course for not wanting to eat any of the fattening foods as I worked my way towards losing more. And if we went to special events, like weddings, or showers, again, I would be urged to eat foods I did not wish to and in large portions which I never liked to do anyway. Again, people would look at me strangely and have a remark at the ready, but I was on a mission to lose weight. I wanted to know I was going to be around for my kid and not get sick on them along our journey together.

What I saw around me was a lot of overweight people that ate a lot of sugary or fattening foods and had many health issues, and I did not want to be one of them. Not at such a young age. Not that being overweight is a bad thing, it just did not work well for me at the time. And I'm not talking about people who have health issues that keep them overweight, or life changes, which alter our bodies once again. That's a whole other ball game.

I felt that many of the ailments these people had, like high or low blood pressure, diabetes, swollen ankles, and the list went on, could be because of their lifestyle and maybe if they ate healthier, some of those ailments would subside. I was going to at least work at eating smarter and whatever would come, I would at least know in my mind that I had made better choices than what I saw many people doing around me.

After my parent fell ill and I was caring for them, neither my other parent nor myself were eating well. There was so much to do and not enough time to do it in. We did not sleep much, and we were so stressed. Both of us did what we could to keep up with the demands of dealing with my ill parent and all the people coming in and out of the home.

When I noticed I was getting headaches, something I did not suffer much from at all, and that I was losing weight, I turned my attention to my other parent. If I was not stopping to eat well, then I was sure neither were they. Most of my time had been concentrating on looking after my ill parent, especially when we first got them home and the other parent was so independent that I did not pay as much attention as I probably should have. But it is also easier to see things clearer in hindsight.

My ill parent had to have their foods prepared special, so aside from making that food for them, I often brought food upstairs for my other parent, thinking they were eating it, but I would find it still in the fridge days later, waiting for me to bring it back down to my family. My parent did not wish to burden me to look after them as well since they were still capable of looking after themselves. They also felt guilty to take my food and would leave it there, insisting I bring it back to feed my child.

It was not that they did not like my food, as they ate it all the time, they just felt guilty having me cook for them too, with everything else that was going on. But we were a family and we all had to take care of each other. Now was not the time to feel guilty or embarrassed their kid was cooking for them.

They would usually grab some bread and fruit and that would be lunch, or dinner and I had to put a stop to this. So, I made some changes and insist they eat better, and believe me did I get push back. When one is so fiercely independent it is hard to take help from others, but this was going to be a lesson for them to accept the help from me, their daughter, who was very willing to cook for them.

This is one of those situations that I was talking about where illnesses affect everyone, not just the person you care for, so you have to keep an eye on everyone. It is not easy to do, depending on what is going on and you can have your hands full. For me, even though I checked in with that parent constantly, and I thought they were eating the foods I was bringing to them, they were not. Yet they kept assuring me they were fine in the food department which I knew otherwise. They were going through their own emotional turmoil and did not wish to burden me.

I had to literally, stop my parent from doing all the other things they found they had to do around the house, instead of eating and sit them down at the table, joining them as they ate. At least that way, I could ensure they had put food in their mouth. Many times, they would push the food aside, finding some other excuse to not eat yet, like having to go and fold the clothes at that moment, after the laundry buzzard had just chimed, or the house needed cleaning right then and there because so and so was going to come to visit and the house had to look spotless. Which, believe me, it did. Plus, they would refuse to eat unless my ill parent had already eaten and was resting or asleep for the night. I know they just needed something to keep them busy and take their mind off what else was going on, but it actually, stressed me out, even more, having to look after them in this way.

We had to get special equipment in for my ill parent and learn how

to use it safely. There were still therapists, personal support workers, and the like, coming to help us throughout the day. For the first few months, our front door was a revolving one and frankly, I do not think it stopped. I had my health issues and my own family to care for, plus now as I said, I had the added stress of having to make sure both parents were looked after and a huge responsibility. If something happened to either one of them, everyone would be taking it out on me.

There was special food to make for my ill parent, food for my healthier parent, food for my family, and other foods for me since I had developed a lot of food sensitivities. There were more chores to do, with cleaning and laundry and lots of drama as everybody got used to the new normal in our household. If you can call it getting used to such a life change as we had.

So, to make things easier for me, since I was not sleeping much and the days and nights were long, I started making bigger batches of food. If I made soups, I made a lot and froze them. I bought vegetables that were already cut up, instead of peeling and cutting them up fresh, which was the way I used to do things. If I made cutlets, I breaded them ahead of time and froze them, that way, all we had to do was fry them when we were ready to have them. I made batches of the special food for my ill parent and froze those containers too, not more than a weeks' worth, so that it was as fresh as it can be, and we always had food ready. But I made sure to make fresh foods as often as I could through the week, given the time at hand. Because that was what my parent was used too. Believe it or not, I even kept baby food on hand, for my ill parent, just in case the electricity went out and we had one of those fancy fish warmer trays that I actually, ended up using to warm up their food once when the electricity did indeed go out for a full day. Talk about being prepared. Or was it being paranoid? Remember, my ill parent's food had to be blended to a particular consistency to swallow. I had to make sure I had a backup plan.

My healthier parent's breakfast consisted of coffee and cookies, which was a staple in our European household, so I tried to make them eat healthier, but they were so used to eating this way that they were happy. So, I had to make sure lunches and dinners were more nutritious. Whether they ate it or not was up to them in the end.

Even though we knew we had to eat well and keep ourselves hydrated, when you are stressed and have so much going on, it is difficult to stay on track. I was so tired that I would not do either the way I knew I should and often skipped meals. Once I noticed my energy levels depleting and noticed my healthier parent was not eating well either I knew I had to change something for us both.

As difficult as it is when you are taking care of someone and your time is not your own, you must strive to eat healthily. It will get your energy levels up and allow you to better care for yourself and your loved ones. Make your meals as healthy as possible, given the time you have on your hands. Think of your own creative ways to put food together that will benefit your entire family. Continue to watch other members, especially those that are also caring for loved ones, as well as the elderly, because it is so easy to not eat right. Illness can come about rather quickly, and you certainly do not want another person to look after.

Food makes us and it also can break us if we are not having what our bodies need to stay strong. So, make an extra effort to get healthier foods on the table, and don't be afraid to employ another family member to help too so you are not going crazy doing everything yourself. You can make a schedule and one person can cook one time and another person at another or make it fun and work together. It just takes the stress off everyone.

Remember you can order food in, now but make sure you are ordering from places where you can make healthy choices. And don't forget to find out the ingredients of what's in that food. This is one reason why I would rather make things myself. I know what goes in them, from the oils I prefer like grapeseed, avocado, or coconut, to the types of salts such as Himalayan, as well as I can change up the number of spices I wish to add to things. And if I want to bread something, I no longer use breadcrumbs which bother me but substitute with different kinds of nut flours like almond or coconut flour or even garbanzo, better known as chickpea flour.

If you cannot get those nutritious foods in you there are different dietary supplements, even protein powders for shakes, that are on the market to get more protein in you or greens for example. Something many do not like to eat. But always, and I mean always check with your doctor first to find out what works best for you and what does not, because some dietary supplements can have unwanted side effects when taking other prescription drugs with them, or there may be other reasons not to take certain supplements that may not agree with you.

But if you get the green light from your doctor there are certainly many supplements to choose from, so again, be cautious and do your research of what brands you buy. Some may be better for you than others. Some like liquids may absorb faster than a pill, for example.

There are many vitamins on the market of course, like vitamin B, vitamin D, magnesium, calcium, probiotics, digestive enzymes, or even pills you can take if you are lactose intolerant. It just depends on what you are looking to improve. And there are a lot of good Naturopathic doctors out there that can help you navigate things and choose the right vitamins for your body. Again, check things out with your doctors first.

There are a lot of other nutritional supplement products on the market that you may often see seniors drink, so just look at what seems healthier for you and your family. For me, I like to buy protein powders from the Health store and make my own drink. Maybe even make some smoothies, adding other healthy products. I find some drinks have a lot of sugar, which does not bode well for me.

Also, check with your pharmacists, as some of these drinks for seniors are covered by government programs. At least they are in Ontario, Canada, at the time of writing this. Ask for the forms and fill them out if you qualify. In our case, the pharmacist filled them out, with a portion to be filled by our family doctor and we were able to offer them to my ill parent to strengthen them.

Some people eat to their body type or their blood type, and you can certainly do some research on each and speak to your doctor to get more information. If you are eating for your body type, you may wish to find out which type you are first, so you understand how your body works and how to strengthen it and or eat depending on what you wish to accomplish. Are you a banana type, long and lean, have an hourglass shape, or is your body more like an apple, round all around? By the way, these types pertain to men and women.

A banana type or ectomorph body type is naturally long and lean and has a hard time gaining muscle. Not to say that they cannot, it is just harder for this shape. They generally have narrow shoulders and hips. They tend to have a fast metabolism. Those with an hourglass figure or mesomorph type have broad shoulders, are narrow in the waist and hips, and are muscular, compact, and athletic. It is easy for them to put on muscle, but also easy to not see when they have gained weight, since they usually put it on proportionally, throughout their entire body. Endomorph types are soft, round, pudgy, and overweight.

If you eat to your blood type, you may want to know if your blood type is, O, A, B or AB. Again, check with your doctor before you change things too much. Remember, you are already going through stressful times, do not overdo things unless you are comfortable with the changes you wish to make. Also remember, that eating for your body or blood type is not for everyone. There are pros and cons and different information for each.

Here is what I found regarding eating for your blood type. And by the way, there are some fabulous books on this way of eating. If you are type O, it is best to eat a high-protein diet, heavy on lean meat, poultry, fish, and vegetables, and light on grains, beans, and dairy. Various supplements are good to help with any troubles with your tummy and other issues some O types tend to have.

For those with type A blood, meat may not be the best for you. Stick to fruits and vegetables, beans and legumes, and whole grains. Try and eat organic and fresh foods as type A blood types tend to have sensitive immune systems.

Those that have a B blood type may be best to avoid corn, wheat, buckwheat, lentils, tomatoes, peanuts, and sesame seeds. Chicken may also not agree with them. Green vegetables, eggs, certain meats, and low-fat dairy are fine.

AB blood types may do well with tofu, seafood, dairy, and green vegetables. AB types may have low stomach acid and may wish to avoid caffeine, alcohol, and smoked or cured meats.

Wheatgrass is something else you can try to get your energy levels up, for anyone who likes to try something natural. It has some amazing healing properties, and it has always given me the energy I needed to go that much further in my day. It does have an earthy, bitter taste to it, so you need to brace yourself the first time you take it, but you do become accustomed to the taste with time.

It was something that I had stumbled on several years ago but never knew of any nutritional stores close to me that sold the juice. I eventually found a place that carried the powder, and I would mix it with some water and drink it. At one point I even found the seeds and started growing a small plant at home.

Fast forward to today, you can find it a lot easier now and I like to keep frozen cubes I purchase, in my freezer. It is good to take daily. I even bought a masticating juicer, with an auger, so that I could make my own juice from the wheatgrass I was growing and started juicing fresh vegetables, feeling the amazing energy they would give my body. If someone told me a few years before, that I would be eating, well, in this case drinking the juice from kale, spinach, beets, cucumber, zucchini, ginger, turmeric, and so many other green vegetables I would never have believed them.

Juicing opened an entire world for me, and I found other nutritional items that were helping me to stay strong, given what I had gone through health-wise. I started making shakes with protein powders, adding chia seeds, hemp hearts, spirulina, and chlorella, and learned so much more about other foods that I found all contributed to me staying strong.

Keep in mind not to keep freshly squeezed juices in your fridge for too long as they lose many of their nutrients the longer you keep them, which defeats the purpose of what you are trying to do. I make enough for two days, drinking about a glass of it fresh. I usually get another glass or two for the following day.

I remember when my kid and I had to travel a distance and given my health at the time, I truly did not know if I could make the trip back home. Just getting there had depleted my energy. I was really worried, to say the least. I tried to rest before starting the trip back home but I was still tired and beside myself on what to do to get us there. I remembered there was a health store nearby. Gathering my strength, I drove straight there, hoping they would have some wheatgrass and praying it would give me the energy to make it back.

Sure, enough they had small amounts of the juice they were selling and even though it was expensive, I bought a small cup. More like a couple of ounces. I remember feeling the bitter taste of the wheatgrass as it went down my throat. I felt a rush through my body as I swallowed it. But to me, it was like medicine. I bought a small plant knowing I had to make the same trip for the next month and every day, I would literally, wrap some of the wheatgrasses in a paper towel and sit in my car as I waited for my kid, chewing on this thing to get the juice out and discarding the rest. I am sure if anyone would have seen me, which believe me, I tried hard not to have happened, they would have thought I was a mad cow, wanting my grass fix.

It is funny when I think of it now, but it has quickly given strength back to other family members after surgeries, along with my crazy concoctions of vegetable juicing. I know now that whenever I am feeling more run down than normal, I take a bit more wheatgrass for the day and I feel that much better, faster.

Eat with love and do not rush your meals. Make sure you chew your food well so that the digestion process is easier for your body. And do not lie down right after eating as you may begin to suffer from acid reflux or heartburn. The juices working to digest your foods will move up your esophagus when you lie down too soon, causing you to be uncomfortable.

I try to split my plate up with half of it being vegetables and try to get my protein in there too. That became a little harder once I stopped eating meats. It was beginning to bother me, so I thought I would try to stay away for a while, but I noticed I was not getting enough protein and my nails began to grow weaker and break quickly. They usually were strong. It was all new to me and I'm still learning but I had to try to get my proteins in other foods, whereas in the past, I would just throw some meat, spices, and vegetables together and call it a day.

I know, not every meal will have the recommended food groups because first of all, we want to live and we will have our cheat days, and secondly, life changes every day. You may not be home and have to eat whatever you have available, such as when you are visiting others, or what happened to us when we were at the hospital with my ill parent. So we packed lunches in the morning before leaving for the hospital. That way we could at least have some decent food we liked. Try and work towards having more days than not where you are eating better and continue until it becomes a lifestyle, not a diet or just a change you don't stick to, because you will ultimately, get back to eating the old way which is what you may have worked so hard to change.

As difficult as it is these days with all the distractions around us, try to eat with the television off and stay away from your computer or phone so you can concentrate on your eating and how the food makes you feel. When you eat slower instead of gulping the food down, you will not overeat and you will recognize when you are no longer hungry, instead of eating just because a certain portion is on your plate.

A good thing to get used to also is to drink some water about half an hour before your meals as it helps in the digestion process. Sometimes drinking water when you think you are hungry will stop your hunger and it could be your body telling you to keep it hydrated. You can start to get hunger pains, headaches, maybe even have difficulty concentrating all because your body needs some water.

So, the next time you hear your tummy grumbling, and you have already had a good meal, or your mealtime is getting closer, have a drink of water and see if that helps you to feel better. Then proceed to eat your regular meal, and watch the snacking, which can catch us off guard, because we all know how easy it is to go through a bag of chips, and before we know it the bag is empty, and you are the only one that has been eating from it all week.

Stay as healthy as you can and do not be afraid to try something new. Mind the time you have of course when you are making meals, but the more you feed your body with good foods, the more energy you will have and the better you will feel. That of course translates to being able to handle more things throughout your day. Try and get some exercise, maybe go for a walk, and get some fresh air. Go into nature if you can. Moods will improve and who knows, you may even lose a few pounds and get the rest of your family healthy too.

Adding some movement in your day so your body stays strong helps to keep you feeling younger and may even keep some aches and pains away. Being more active may allow you to enjoy doing more things, like going for walks, running, bike rides, or working out. Just keeping the body moving if you can so you do not get weak.

If you have various ailments you have to watch out for then as always, speak to your doctor first before you start any exercises and find out what you can and cannot do, given your health. As a caregiver, you have a lot of work to do and maybe even some lifting here and there, so if that is the case, keeping yourself stronger is important, so that you have the strength and stamina to keep doing what you need to do and not injure yourself as you try to maybe lift someone. Remembering of course to take your rest time when your body calls for it.

If I didn't have the time to work out the way I was used to when I was younger and healthier, I would incorporate movements throughout my day. If I was watching television, I was on the floor stretching and moving my legs, doing sit-ups, or arm circles, side bends, something. Whatever struck me at the moment I would do, since my time was limited. After I fell ill and was not able to do what I could before, I modified my movements. Oftentimes, I would even put on my old CDs to get motivated by the people working out in them, but I would go at my own pace. That was good enough for me at certain times in my life. If you can, try to bring along some friends and family as it not only can be more fun, but it gets them exercising too.

During the pandemic, as many of you know, we were not able to get together with other households and many stores, restaurants and more, were closed. Not being able to go to the gyms meant many people could not work out and some had a hard time keeping in shape at home. But for those that tried, I heard so many stories of friends and family members who found it expensive to purchase items to work out at home, given how much the prices had risen through this time. I had my trusted CDs, plus with another friend, we got into a rhythm that we would call each other at a certain time of the day and walk together. Each one of us would be at our own homes, and we would just talk on the phone as we would walk our own neighborhoods. Before we knew it, both of us had walked a good distance, getting our exercise in for the day. Even walking your dog is good to get out and get some fresh air.

For those of you that don't have equipment at home to work out in, but wish to keep your muscles strong, (after checking with your doctor of course, given health issues), fill some water jugs and use them as weights. Or put some cans in a bag that is not going to break on you and you can use them to lift, up and down. Again, use common sense and be careful not to swing them so they hit you on the head or injure someone else.

Pick up some exercise rubber bands you can order online or get in your neighboring stores, to use in your workout routine. Do sit-ups and crunches on the floor or use a chair or bench. Just make sure the chair is not going to tip over and you are safe. Crunches can also be done in many other ways, like using your body weight and crunching side to side as you lift each leg. You can research other ways too.

Go up and down the first step or more, on your staircase or in your hallway of an apartment, to get your heart moving and your legs and arms pumping. If you don't have steps where you live, see if you can purchase an exercise stepper. You may also be able to go outside if the weather is fine and find a place that has steps you can jog up. If you are creative, you will find a way.

You can use either a mat or a carpet when you do routines on the floor. Push-ups can be done on the wall or floor. I remember when I was younger, using my kitchen counter to work my arms and tummy. I would be facing outwards and lifting myself off the counter, working my arms, then add the legs to get a good crunch for the tummy. Oh, how I wish I could still do that.

If you do not wish to use items for weights, you do not have to. There are so many videos online of people you can follow to even just do some stretches or other gentle movements, so your body stays strong. Yoga is another great way to stay limber and Tai Chi is something else you can look into. Why do you want to stay in shape? Aside from the many health benefits? Because you may try and lift someone you are caring for and hurt yourself. And you certainly do not want to do that. Plus, you will notice you will feel stronger in your arms, legs, and your entire body, allowing you to do more. And you will also notice your clothes will fit much nicer. Staying fit may not be for everyone but just try and keep your body moving, even if it's just a simple enjoyable walk, and let others do the heavy lifting if it's not for you.

Eating healthy is a choice and you have to want to do it, otherwise, you will not make wise choices, but I am sure that if you change your eating habits to a healthier living, if you are already not doing so, you will feel much better and with the help of your doctors, natural paths, nutritionists and the like, I'm sure they can put you on the right path to healthy living.

Chapter Four

Simple Step Number 3

Be Patient

When you are a caregiver especially to someone with a mental illness you need to pack a lot of patience. And I mean a lot. You have to have patience with yourself, your family, and certainly patience with those that are not well. The more you have and the calmer you are the easier things will be for everyone. At least that is what I found when I was taking care of my ex-husband. He struggled enough some days trying to cope with everything he was going through. The last thing he needed was someone yelling and screaming or accusing him of doing something out of the ordinary or absurd. Something that to him was as normal as breathing, but to everyone else was just strange and different than how most of us conduct ourselves and what we deem to be normal.

Anytime someone screams and yells, what happens? Well, of course, the other person does the same and before you know it you all can get pretty angry over a small incident that you really, did not need to get so upset over. And given the fact that some people cannot control their actions, can you really, get angry at them? I can hear you screaming, "Yes!', as you read my words. I know, it's hard not to sometimes, but that's where self-control really, comes into play as well as understanding what is going on with your loved one.

If you know what is bothering them and why they are acting out or acting strangely it may help you to figure out how to help them. They may be upset because they missed an important event or forgot to do something, and so they are blaming themselves for not being on top of a situation. They may just be overcome with emotions and don't know why they are upset.

All they may need is an ear to listen to them and calm them down, talk things out, so you must stay strong during this time. You cannot be crying along with them or yelling and screaming and telling them to get their act together. Remember, if it's a mental illness they are battling, they are coping with a lot of emotional turmoil. So, they will not be thinking straight. They may have a chemical imbalance which can make it difficult for them to control what they are feeling. But they may turn to you for support. They need to know they can trust you and there is a safe zone with you. It is very important for them to feel loved. Otherwise, you may have a bigger problem on your hands.

It really can be any number of reasons why they are feeling the way they are and if you just take some time to talk to them and hear them out, you may be able to get them past the present phase they are dealing with. Then again you may not be able to help at all and may need to get them to a professional that can assist them better. We are not always going to have all the answers or be equipped to get them through all their challenges. Their medications may not be working as their bodies become immune to them, or they are so emotional that it's too big a situation for you to handle.

It's not easy listening to your loved ones freaking out over anything. We all want to be happy and want our loved ones to be too. We may not have signed up for this caregiving role that somehow has fallen to our doorstep, and we cannot just walk away. Maybe the powers that be, have put you in charge of this person and you will have to take a deep breath, stay strong and help how and where you can. Other than that, you cannot do any more than you are. We are only human after all.

When I was with my ex-husband, I tried to understand what he was going through so that I could help ease the emotional rollercoaster he was feeling on any given day. I had to keep the stress away from him and not give my ex-husband too much to deal with. Can you imagine the way you feel when you have had too much to drink, or you are not feeling well? Everything is amplified and you may not wish to deal with certain situations. Other situations may not seem as important.

Well, when someone has a mental disposition noise can seem louder and confusion can set in quickly, given the extra things they have to deal with, and they will shut down or go into an emotional rollercoaster if things get too much for them to handle. Do you really, want to give someone you love more headaches and make them feel worse than they probably already do by not giving them the support they need?

Not that it is any comparison, but I experienced a little bit of that brain overload feeling and sensitivity to noise, this past year when I fell flat on my face and got a concussion. It was a doozie and took months for me to heal. I had to stay away from electronics, lights and I was in slow motion for some time before

I started feeling even close to myself. So, my days were difficult, but my nights were something different.

I was not focusing well of course, so it took a while for me to figure out that propping my pillow up would help the nauseous feeling I would get. I would close my eyes, hoping sleep would come but it was nowhere to be found. The worst was how my brain could not stop thinking of things and felt like it was on fire. I could feel the tingling at the back of my head.

My thoughts were going a hundred miles an hour and I could not stop them even though I tried. Even meditating did not help at first. At times I would focus on little things that kept me thinking about them for what I am sure were hours. I wondered if some of these symptoms were things my ex-husband would experience. I felt this way for a short time, but he would feel his symptoms all the time, and not just months, but years, with days on end, when he would be worse than other days. I commend him on the strength he had, for the most part, to hold it all together as well as he did and keep functioning through everything he was feeling and going through.

It was always a lesson in patience with my ex-husband. Patience with the things he said and did, patience to help him work through his emotional pains, and patience as we would sit together and talk about the things that were getting him down. We would work through his emotions and the other discussions that did not make sense so, I tried to help him understand better. I had to stay level-headed as not only were these times emotional, but I also had my young child to take care of through it all and there were certain times I did not want them to see the emotional upsets. Expressing emotions, I feel is healthy, so that the child gets a feel for real life and can handle situations in their own lives as they grow, but they did not have to witness everything. That was for sure.

Sometimes it would take days for my ex-husband to bounce back from when he did not feel well, sometimes longer as he would putter around the house. I would ask if he would want to go see the doctor, but he would not want to go, feeling more comfortable at home, trying to sleep things off. So, I let him be, knowing he was able to manage his emotions as we worked together with me constantly checking on him. We went for many walks which I found helped both of us and we would sometimes put our child in the wagon, and everyone would get some fresh air, discussing things as we went along with my ex-husband.

There were many tireless nights where I stayed awake with him, yet most people would give in and leave, not putting up with all the nonsense or let them work things out themselves, especially after having to deal with things for a long time. This can be difficult for your loved ones, who may need your support and rationality. Especially, if they are losing touch with reality. There were other nights I stayed awake, wondering how else I could help my ex-husband and I felt this guilt that I was not doing enough for him. I just wanted to find the correct remedy that would bring the man I loved back to some form of normalcy. But I had to have patience with him, and I was grateful to be able to continue as long as we did together as a family.

It takes constant care and supervision when you have someone you know that has a mental illness and it can be a long journey so be prepared to deal with a lot of varying days.

Your patience may wear thin with loved ones over the years, as you all go through so many things to live a decent life and a stable one. Accept how they are and do not blame them for their disposition. Do not hate them, or make them feel unwanted or unloved, because let's face it, now it might be several years that you have been dealing with this all and you are exhausted. Some loved ones may need extra attention over the years that you cannot continue to provide given the family dynamics, or as you all age, and or have your health issues to deal with too, so there is a lot to consider as time goes on.

Every situation of course is different, but the better days can turn to worse days, medications may have to be revisited and maybe changed altogether. Or the person's emotions get so out of wack that it is like they need a reset to the brain. So, you may find yourself heading back to the hospital hoping to get them further help to keep your loved one calm, so they do not hurt themselves, or others.

When you are dealing with someone who has a mental disposition and they are in psychosis, their brain is affected even more than on regular days, so it becomes that much harder for them to process situations well. They get out of touch with reality and become delusional. They may even hear voices.

You as the caregiver, family member, or friend, must understand as I mentioned earlier, that person's brain is not thinking straight. They cannot help the way they are feeling nor the things they may do or say. It is all part of what they are going through, so they need lots of love and understanding from those around them. They need guidance, direction, and help to get them medical attention in hopes of stabilizing their condition. They may not realize how unstable and out of touch with reality they are.

At times, patience is required, over the process of getting your loved ones the proper help, they need with the institutions and services around you that could help to stabilize or heal them. This can take time depending on the severity of the illness and what stage your loved one is at.

What can also take time is helping to let your loved one understand that they do have a situation that needs tending to. They may not feel there is anything wrong with them and refuse help. They may even turn away from you, thinking you are out to get them, when in fact you are only trying to help. If you can, depending on the severity of their symptoms, give them the space they need to realize that they should seek further medical attention. Remember, that if you are dealing with those that are underage it will be you that will have to make the decisions as they of course are not legally able to, and you are responsible for them, but still remember to deal with their emotions delicately as they may not understand where you are taking them and why you are heading to a doctor or hospital.

Do keep in mind, however, that at some point, younger or older, you may be the one that needs to take the necessary action in finding your loved one the help they need to heal. As I say all these things, please remember that I am not a doctor and speak only from experiences. So, please consult with your doctors, family members, and those you trust and know can give you the right advice to help you help your loved ones and keep you sane in the process.

You want to find the right people that can get your loved ones through any roadblocks or red tape when navigating the institutions that can provide help to them. Look for the right place to take them to if they need to be assessed and or require further medical attention. Search for the right doctors that understand your loved one's situation and mental disposition and can help you get through some difficult times. That way you and your loved ones are not left to figure things out on your own which can be a daunting task. If you do not find them the first time you look, do not give up. They are out there and if you want to find them, they will show up.

It can sometimes feel all so overwhelming when you are already exhausted in dealing with your loved one and you do not know if you can go much further, yet, you know you must find other information or doctors to help them. You may also wish to find someone that can assist you to keep moving forward, like a trusted family member or friend that you can bounce things off of, or a phycologist, psychoanalyst, or psychiatrist for you to speak to and keep your mind straight.

Some people may spend years, helping their loved ones, trying to stay sane and balanced, as well as anyone else in the family that is having a difficult time dealing with this all. Where do you begin is a big question? Do you go to the family doctors to help you and or your family? And can they help your loved one who is suffering from a mental challenge? Or do you go to the hospitals? And which ones have the availability or the knowledge you are comfortable with knowing they can help, given their circumstances? Who else is out there that can assist? What are the proper steps each institution follows?

For example, at the time of writing this, if you think your loved one needs to be assessed further than say what the local doctor or hospital can help with, and your loved one is back home, they may not be eligible to go to another institution that you may feel can help them further because they are home. They must go from institution to institution. And only if they are eligible since there may be other people that need more medical attention than your loved one does and therefore, they get moved ahead of the line so to speak. Having said that, if your loved one does not get the proper help soon, their mental sanity can deteriorate, when they could have been helped earlier on when symptoms were first realized, not to mention, that none of us want our loved ones to feel insecure and unstable at any time.

If you have taken your loved one to the doctor or hospital because you know something is not right with their mental state of mind they may be spoken to or assessed by the doctors. They may deem your loved ones stable enough to be back out in society. That is great and all so wonderful, but you get your loved one home and realized not much has changed, so now you must keep a close eye on them at this point, because they may not be ready to go out on their own again. Remember, you are with them all the time. You know them well. The doctors have just seen them for a few minutes, or even if it is a few days. So, to them, your loved one may be good enough to release from the hospital. But remember how I said my ex-husband used to fool the doctor's all the time?

This is where you may have to step in and make a stronger case for your loved ones to ensure they get the medical attention they need. Do not give up. Persevere. I have seen it all too often in the past, and not just with my ex-husband's case, where the person with a mental disposition, is kept in the hospital for a day or if lucky, even a few days to be assessed, and then released. Or the individual can discharge themselves if they do not want to be there. Yet, they are still not well, and their mental state of mind has not changed enough to warrant them being discharged. But they do not pose a threat to society or themselves, so they are released. Yet, you know that hours ago, that was not the case.

If this all sounds confusing, it is. Believe me, it is not a cut-and-dry situation. There can be a lot of hoops to jump through and hopefully, you can get steered in the right direction. We, unfortunately, were not with my ex-husband, and his situation just kept getting worse. Yes, it was a long time ago, but as I have said many times before, it has not changed much even to this day.

I wish I had more answers on how to navigate the system better, but the amount of help can depend on the severity of the disposition, and each town, city, country, institution, can have its way of dealing with mental illness. Each case is also unique, so reach out to the medical experts in your communities for help, and do not be afraid to question things or research further for more information and help. It is out there. You may have to look deeper for it.

The family doctor is usually a good start and if you or your loved ones are not comfortable with them, look for someone you are all comfortable with. Because if your loved one does not trust that doctor and they prescribe a certain medication or service, your loved one may not follow through with the treatment and could end up worse than they are. And make sure your doctors know the full situation on what is going on so they can treat according to the symptoms or refer you to the right person to help further. Also, ensure your doctor knows all the medications your loved one is taking or any allergies they may have so the doctors do not prescribe something that gives adverse effects.

Regarding the person that is let go from the hospitals when they are still not very stable, this is something I yet do not understand fully. When my ex-husband was discharged the following day after bringing him to the hospital in the condition he was in, they must have treated him overnight with medications, but let him go the following day. They had arranged for him to attend the anger management classes. But he was out of sorts when I went to the house to check up on him, the following day. I wondered what he would retain from the class, given the shape he was in.

I guess I expected that the hospital would monitor him for a few more days to ensure the medications were working to help him and that he would be stable enough to function when he got home. He was back to struggling with his emotions in no time. Bandages are just that, a temporary solution that does not bode well for someone who needs more care when it comes to dealing with the mind.

I had gone to the house expecting to clean up the place and bring him some food for when he would come out of the hospital, but I did not expect it to be the following day. I know I'm no doctor and do not know all the ins and outs of dealing with mental health, so I was upset they did not watch him for a few days to understand his symptoms a little more and help him on a long-term basis. Or at least a few more days to ensure he was seriously ready to go home with his mind in better shape. I was not given time to explain what he was dealing with before the social worker threw me out of the room that day either, and my ex-husband was in no shape to discuss his symptoms in detail.

I say threw me out because that was how it felt. There was no discussion with me to dig deeper as to why my ex-husband was feeling the way he was or what could have prompted these feelings. They came out of the room, after speaking with him and told me to head on home, because they would keep him overnight. I was relieved, thinking we would maybe get to the bottom of this situation, but that thought was short-lived. Then to not call me to pick up my ex-husband concerned me as well, because of course, when I saw him the following day, I did not think his mind was very stable, yet he had been released and was going home where he would be alone. His thoughts could have put him in a bad frame of mind. What if he still felt out of sorts and went off to do someone some harm, or even to himself, given his condition. My ex-husband did not think to call me either to bring him home. I do not know if he took the bus or if the hospital put him in a taxi.

Because I saw my ex-husband's mind still so fragile, I was beside myself on how to help him and where would we go from here. Remember this was a new experience to me and I did not get any counseling from the hospital on what to expect or how to help my ex-husband further, after discharge. I was also so afraid of what shape he was in and if he still felt like harming others.

He spent the next several months alone at home doing his own thing. I would come by every day to check up on him and call throughout the day, until he was ready to move in with family as I had already moved out with our child, realizing how dangerous he could become. I was not going to stick around and have something bad happen when my guard was down. I had already spent the better part of the last five years or so barely sleeping, afraid of what might happen if I fell into a deep sleep. Either to him or us.

I knew that if I would have left sooner, I had better have all my paperwork together so that he did not get custody of our child. He was in no shape for that, and I had to protect our child. Like

I said earlier, pack lots of patience because there may be a lot of emotions and events you may experience where you may not fully understand or know how to deal with best, and this is when it's a good idea to involve others that can help you decide what the next best steps can be for you and your loved ones.

The closest I could come to understand why people who have been taken to the hospital with psychosis but are discharged before they are well, is that first of all, yes, there is a cost to the health care system so they will be discharged once they feel they are mentally stable enough to be on their own and that will not necessarily be when we, ourselves think they are good. The other reason is that if the patient is coherent enough to sign themselves out, they can, or the person assessing them is not understanding the full scope of what is going on with them because of course, they only see them for a brief time. This is why I feel that depending on the situation, would monitoring them for more than a day or two not assist?

With my ex-husband, I had hoped that there would be a follow-up after discharge or other help that could be offered after my ex-husband was released. Something that maybe even our private benefits could help with. Maybe send my ex-husband to a specialist that could deal with him on a longer-term and ensure he was healing. But again, where to begin. And would this mean to start over with any new doctors, instead of the hospital working in tandem with a doctor we would be assigned to after discharge? At least they would have access to tests performed or outcomes of those tests, which of course in turn could move us further ahead instead of behind.

I have heard how even today; the family is not always consulted with to get their take on what goes on at home. Don't get me wrong, there could be cases, where the family member could truly be the problem and want to condemn their loved one who is not well, so I understand the institutions having to watch out for this. But I still believe, rules and many changes must be looked at closer to help those that need medical assistance, and not just to talk to them, but stabilize their psychosis. Guide them for the future so they can live happier.

It can be a vicious circle if your loved ones are never really getting the help, they need to stabilize their mental state of mind and it might be up to you to push the institutions into helping your loved ones become more stable. Because if not, your loved one can fall into psychosis and become out of touch with the world again.

So, if your loved one has been released from a hospital or an institution and is still not well, you begin the process all over again, trying to get them back to the doctor's office or hospital for medical attention. Again, the doctor or hospital may not hear your end of what is going on and seeing that your loved one looks fine or well enough to be back out in society, they are discharged. They may have been given some medication but given the fact that they have not been stabilized, they do not take the medication and they go into psychosis again.

You may even get your loved one stable for a short time, and for different reasons, they may become unbalanced again. It can be because the medication they are on is no longer working well enough for them, it can be because they forgot to take what they were supposed to, be it pills, or go for their injections, or maybe something else is going on and you need to be alert to what is happening so that you can provide them with the attention they need. As I said, this can be a lifelong job and there will ultimately be some things you get used to, like certain ways your loved ones may act that you just let them do their thing and do not mind the strangeness of it all.

But it is their stability you must keep an eye on to make sure they are safe and functioning as best as they can. Keep in mind, when I say that being with someone that has a mental disposition can be a lifelong event, please remember that each situation is different, and you must adjust your life to what you can handle and or remove yourself and others if situations get too uncomfortable or dangerous to be around. Just please, make sure you have been able to get them to the right place to help them, so they are not left alone to fall further behind or hurt themselves or others. Even if you need to do that from afar to keep you safe.

It's not easy for both sides. The person suffering the delusions may think the world is against them, that nobody loves them, and they have been abandoned. The person trying to help them may wonder why this person is acting the way they are, and what they will do next, not understanding that it is a mental illness the person is suffering from and cannot always help what they say or do.

In the beginning, when my ex-husband would do strange things, like get angry at someone parked in a spot they should not be in at the mall or get up and leave the room when some company would come to visit us both; people he usually enjoyed being around, confused me, upset me, then irritated me. I could not understand why he would do the things he did, but as time went on and he began doing more strange things, like putting holes in our walls or painting a room over the wallpaper, something, he knew better than to do, I began to wonder what was going on. Again, strange actions can begin as subtle things, and become increasingly, more severe over time. This is when you question, that their actions are not normal and need to understand what is going on with them.

There were many times I felt like I had a jealous teenager on my hands fighting against our young child, instead of an adult. There were times the television had to be on the station my ex-husband said, even though it was too frightening a show for little ones to watch, and I would have to sternly step in and insist the channel be changed or the television turned off. My nature was always a calm one and I did not like violence or arguing, or raising my voice, so it was a hard thing for me to do given the type of person I was. At the time, I was still trying to understand what was going on in my ex-husband's head and why he would act as he did.

There was one time my ex-husband got a haircut from our young child as he slept. I came home to find them both sporting new styles. Our child found the children's scissors and decided to be a hairdresser for the day. It was funny, but at the same time, I was overly concerned, because our child could have easily left the house or injured themselves while my ex-husband slept. At the time, our child could have been about three years old, so many things could have happened.

I remember being so emotionally drained over having to deal with my ex-husband and his ways and he just kept adding to the things he would do that tested my patience. One year my ex-husband decided to peddle his bike to another city, about four hours or more away. Yes, you read that correctly, by bicycle. He had already suffered a heart attack several years before and was no longer in the shape he used to be in. He also chose to go during a heatwave. The type of temperatures the weatherman warns you to stay inside, because you cannot even breathe, given the hot temperatures and or humidity. For someone in the shape he was in, it was not the best day to have chosen.

I got a call from him asking me to pick him up somewhere on the road, as he could no longer make it further than where he had ended up and I, of course, left work in a hurry, trying to find him as I drove up the way I had hoped he had taken his bike. He had continued to the closest mall and had finally called me to let me know where he was after I had my own adventure trying to locate him.

When I found him, I barely spoke a word. I was worried for his safety, given the sweltering heat and humidity, he had chosen to ride in. It was very unusual for me not to say anything as I was always ready to give a hand, a kind word, and a lot of love. I was a very forgiving person and as I said, there was no point in getting angry because he was going to do the things he was going to do, and I just had to understand it and work with each event as best I could. I was beginning to understand by then, that my ex-husband had more going on than just small bouts of depression. I knew when the time came that I would have had enough, then I guess, I would deal with that too.

All his recent actions were accumulating, and I was reaching a boiling point so, my anger rose as he just stood by and watched me struggle to pick up his heavy bike and put it in the trunk of my car. I had already had the car accident previously and was still not strong enough to lift heavy things, not to mention the pain it gave me. As my ex-husband watched me, he looked like this little kid getting reprimanded by the parent yet, I had not raised my voice to him, nor did I say any derogatory remarks. I was just silent for the most part and I knew he was aware I was angry. I guess that was enough for him to know I was not happy with all that had transpired.

But at that moment, I was so concerned for him, so angry that he would not care for his well-being or even think of us, his family. As you can see, even though we know better, as caregivers, we have our moments as well, where we too are free to feel so many emotions. As hard as we try to keep them in check.

I kept thinking, what if he had suffered another heart attack? I knew his mind was not working right, but it still did not make me feel any better. I was frustrated on how to help him, still upset that he would not listen to me earlier in the day when I told him to take the Go train if he really, wanted to make this trip. I was angry, hurt and so many other emotions that went on inside my head of why I continued to put up with this all. And why I continued to put up with it alone, not pushing him harder to find help. But again, I did not want to upset him on his good days and frankly, his bad days were beginning to concern me on how low he could go that I would not be able to let him understand he needed more help. And as mentioned, if he did not want to go anywhere, my hands were tied to some degree, in having him seek further help.

Thank goodness for the cell phones we had back then and today, as they have become our lifelines to our communications wherever we are. Gone long ago, were the Bell telephone booths we used to have, situated in many places in our cities, but all I kept thinking of with my ex-husband riding an area not well-traveled during the day, was what would have happened if he had not been able to get to his phone or if he were in distress and there would be nobody around to help him?

As I said earlier, I do not like to scream and yell, but that day took all the strength I had to not pack my bags right then and there and take our kid and leave. I had experienced enough of this life, making myself sicker in the process, but at the same time, I had to understand what my ex-husband was going through. Did I stay or did I leave? Did I continue to see this through?

There was so much confusion around that time and every day called on me to stay patient and deal with my ex-husband with love and understanding for what he was going through. It is a hard thing to stay patient when you are so exhausted you cannot think straight, and everything is crumbling around you, but it is still up to you to fix whatever needs fixing because your partner or someone you care for is not stable enough to handle whatever is going on.

For me, I had to build a strong backbone. I was dealing with things on my own, along with caring for my family. My ex-husband was manipulative and impulsive. That was part of his symptoms. If he wanted to accomplish something, he was very determined to follow through one way or another on any ideas that popped in his head. He was always spending money we did not have and there were times I had to stay firm but calm with him.

Like the time he tried to take money out of our kid's account through the instant teller machines. He knew the amount he wanted was not in the account, so he thought he would fool the machine into giving him money. He deposited an empty envelope into the machine but registered that he had deposited a certain dollar amount that he had not put in. Then, he tried to withdraw the cash that was not really there.

I received a call the next day from a bank manager wanting an explanation of what was going on and the woman threatened to take legal action. I was floored my ex-husband would attempt such a thing. Whatever little trust I had left, was gone and since it was my account, I immediately closed it and removed his name from it. That had been an account I had for years and was sad to have to close it, especially given the reason why. The last thing I wanted was a black mark on my kid's account. He was just an innocent child getting thrown under the bus and I was not going to have that.

Another time he wanted to use the funds from the sale of our house to buy a bowling alley in town that had gone bankrupt. He did not know the first thing about running a business, nor would he have the patience for it. We were selling the house because we were downsizing given that he was not working. Even his mother came to me worried when she heard him talking about his plans. I assured my mother-in-law; I was not about to let that happen. My ex-husband was constantly, creating havoc and waiting for someone else to clean it up or bail him out and how could you get angry with him, when he did not understand at times what he was doing? So, when I say pack all the patience you have, I mean it.

Remember to find an outlet for yourself that will help you to keep your cool. Either it is a hobby, speaking to someone who understands what you are going through, or that you trust, going for a walk, meditation; whatever will help you cope with everything you have to juggle, and as always, reach out your hand for help when things get too much for even you to handle.

When I was caring for my ill parent, the patience I needed was not only juggling all the added work that had to get done but also in learning how to care for someone in my ill parent's disposition without losing my mind from exhaustion, stress, and a pile of other emotions that comes with caring for your loved ones at home.

As caregivers, we are not nurses or trained in caring for others, so there was a lot to learn and a lot of people coming and going from the house to teach us things. I remember intently, watching the nurses at the hospital tend to my ill parent so that I would know what to do when we got them home.

There is also a certain amount of patience one needs with the hospitals. They are all so overworked and understaffed and have many government rules to follow. We had some amazing people that looked after my ill parent but having said that there were others, that made us shake our heads in wonder and it made me glad we came every day to be there for my ill parent.

So given what we had seen and experienced, when people asked me why we would spend so much time at the hospital, given that there were nurses and PSW's there to tend to them, I would tell them plainly, that my parent was still surviving because we had been there. We had offered love, but we had also offered an extra pair of eyes and much-needed help, to make sure my ill parent was looked after and were able to call for assistance, right away when we needed to, instead of nobody being available when disaster struck and could have possibly taken my ill parent away to heaven sooner than was their time. And believe me, we had a few close calls.

It was challenging to be on call 24/7, day in and day out when we returned home with my ill parent. There were no sick days off. It didn't matter how we felt, we had to always be alert and there was no one other than my other old and ailing parent and myself.

If my parent felt cold, I would cover them up or take the blankets off if they were too hot. These were things they could no longer do for themselves. All the pillows we used to help with blood flow, as informed to us by the hospital, had to be placed in a specific position and made comfortable for my ill parent since they would stay that way most of the night or when going down for naps. The bed needed to be raised or lowered depending on what was going on.

We could not move my parent or their bed too quickly as it could make them dizzy. Plus, they were going through their own turmoil, once they recovered enough to understand what had happened to them. I tried my hardest to accommodate as best I could with all the love in my heart. I was often rewarded with a smile when everything would come into place, and they could rest comfortably.

There were many sleepless nights, going up and down the stairs to check on my parent, upon hearing them call out. We had to be on top of a lot of health checks that could cause discomfort or bring on other ailments. Equipment had to work properly, and batteries to that equipment had to be charged to work when we needed it. Patience was needed to keep a level head and not go crazy trying to juggle everything we were learning and all we had to get done.

We also needed to know how the equipment worked in every way. I remember one time when a PSW came to the house to help move my parent back in bed for their afternoon nap, using our hydraulic lift. She accidentally touched the emergency switch to stop it from lifting my parent out of the wheelchair and they hung suspended in mid-air, crying in fear. They were not the only ones afraid.

I expected the worker should have known what to do in this instance since we had been told she was trained in how to use the machine, but she did not know and so panic set in. We could not leave my parent hanging and we also had to be careful the machine would not tip from the weight. We had to do something right away.

I also had my healthier parent on the side, who was trying very hard to stay calm, but I could see how frightened they were as was I.

As I quickly checked the machine to figure out what was wrong and what to do next, we were blessed to have a relative visiting, and they suggested to move my parent over the hospital bed and lift it, hoping the bed would rise high enough to get my parent out of the harness of the lift and safely in bed. We got lucky that day as it worked, and after getting my parent down and settled in, I went back to look at the machine. There had to be a reason for it stopping and we had to figure out if it was broken.

I realized the emergency button had been pushed, something we were not told about when we had purchased it from the company. I had been cautious to make sure the unit had always been charged and working fine, but after that incident, I was even more cautious to ensure that button was not touched in error again. I also insisted that other PSW's did not raise my parent so high up on the lift, as not only did it frighten them, but if something went wrong again, we would not have too high a height to work with.

Believe me, when you are looking at your parent's faces as they cry out in fear and they cannot help themselves, suspended in mid-air and you are helpless to help them too, it is a scary thing and pulls at the heartstrings. There was no way we were going to be able to lift my parent out of the harness, given the lack of strength everybody there had that day and the position and height they were at. It would have been a dangerous undertaking I did not want to do.

That incident led me to look at my parent's hospital bed and how we could manually move it to the various positions if the electricity to the house would go out. There was no way to manually move it and so, much to my other parent's wishes against it, I called the company to get an emergency battery installed. Even if I had to pay for it myself, that battery was going to be put in. I was not going to leave things to chance.

I was surprised at my parent that they would not agree to have the battery installed but I also understood all the money that had been spent and was still being spent to make sure my ill parent had the necessary equipment needed to care for them at home. To my other parent, this extra battery seemed unnecessary but to me, it seemed very important. Again, I did not want to leave things to chance. The cost was not a big one at all, so it was going in, no matter what. But you want to talk about patience? My parent sat near the installer as he put the battery on the bed, complaining how this was a waste of money. I had to keep my parent far enough away from the man so as not to bother him or have him wonder what my parent was saying about the ordeal in our language.

The next day, we heard a loud crash and my kid raced up the stairs two at a time, as I followed at a much slower pace, behind them. As we looked out the front window of the house, a car had crashed into the electrical box across the street, cutting off the power to some of our homes. The driver was thankfully not hurt. I just looked at my other parent and walked away saying how glad I was that we had the battery on the bed. My ill parent understood what I said, and we shared a secret smile as they nodded at me, as if to say, a job well done.

There was a lot of patience needed to handle my healthier parent, who was having a difficult time adjusting to watching the love of their life be bedridden and life change for all of us really. There were many times I was challenged by them, and other family members and boy did I feel like yelling and screaming then but I had to keep my cool as best I could because we were all adjusting to the changes. Not to say there were not any screaming matches, because there were plenty with my patience being tested repeatedly. There were many times I had to leave the house to keep the temperature down.

Then there was the patience we had to have with the PSW's that came to the house to help us or the companies that did not have anyone available to come, during a scheduled time, and the help was very desperately needed. Who would help to lift my parent into their chair? Who would help me with the other things I could not do, given my health issues? There were days we would be so upset having to leave my ill parent in bed all day because of the lack of assistance. And I had to make sure that I had someone available to help move my parent back into bed for their afternoon much-needed nap and the nighttime. If one of the PSW's didn't show up, I would be in big trouble.

I remember the one person that almost dropped my ill parent while moving them from the bed to their wheelchair and I had to muster up all my strength to speak calmly and correct the situation quickly as my ill parent cried in fear knowing they were not positioned well in the chair. The worker continued to remove the harness from the lift, but my parent was mostly off the chair which meant once the harness was removed, they would slide to the floor. It took a lot of self-control to deal with some of the workers and this could have ended badly. I also had to stay calm to not upset my ill parent as they were already feeling traumatized for that evening.

I contacted the company that the person worked for and insisted they no longer come to the house. But many of the people that came were professionals, loving, and caring people and I thank them to this day for all the help they gave us. They were wonderful and loving, understanding of my parent's needs and these are traits not only the ill person needs but so does the caregiver living with that person because we have enough on our plates without having to worry about another thing and knowing you can walk out of the room and your loved ones will be cared for is comforting.

I share these stories to remind you that we are all human and given what goes on, we can all lose our cool, but when you are dealing with certain situations, wasting time on getting angry only makes things worse, so instead of getting upset, spend your energy to do what must be done. Stay calm for your health and those of your loved ones. Again, tempers will flare. It's only natural given all that you have to handle, but for the most part, try to keep a level head. A calmer environment will always beat out a crazy one and you will find people easier to deal with if things are handled more calmly.

I know it can be difficult to keep your patience at times but try as hard as you can to make life go smoother for you and everyone else. As I mentioned, you can go for your walks to calm yourself down. That was something I found myself doing a lot. At least in the warmer months. Sometimes even in our cold Canadian winters, I would go out for a few minutes. The cold would wake me up and calm me down.

I had to be in nature, and it would soothe me. I would look at the majestic trees and how even the ones that had toppled over or gone through the harsh winter months, had other parts of the tree growing through them as the warmer months approached. It was like a new life beginning. It was still surviving. I would pass owners walking with their dogs and see how happy the dogs were, wagging their tails, running around a park, free and content with life's simple pleasures. I remember reading how you could put your feet on the ground, touching the grass, or the soil to ground yourself to the Earth. I tried it once because of course, I had to test it out. It worked. At least for me. It calmed me down and got me looking around at the beauty I was surrounded by. Or I just had to look up to the sky and get lost in the moving clouds or the night stars.

If you are new to meditation and you are finding it difficult to quiet your mind from the chatter that keeps going, try putting on some quiet music that will soothe you. When I first started to meditate, I could not quiet my mind and I would try it for about 5 minutes and give up. The next time I would try a little longer. I found soothing music online that would relax me and there are plenty of meditation videos to choose from. There are also plenty of amazing, inspirational leaders out there to assist.

At times, I would recite the Lord's prayer repeatedly, stopping after each sentence. I would take in several deep breaths and repeat the verses. Then I would work at visualizing what it was that I wanted to achieve. Maybe it was to have strength for the following day. Maybe it was blessings I would send to my family. I would visualize a bubble of love going from me to them, moving through the house and blessing the space as it floated to my loved ones. I know, strange, but the idea of sending them my love relaxed me.

You can put on some music and dance or find something that brings you laughter and joy because it will help to brighten you up. Some people love to walk, run, or work out and that has a lot of benefits too. Remember to understand what everyone is feeling. It is not just you who are going through whatever stresses. Everyone else has stuff they are going through too.

Speaking of stresses, if you are so inclined to do, keep a journal by your bedside, writing down all the things that upset you in the pages. This is just a way to release your anger and frustrations. Then, if you like, you can ripe out those pages and throw them away, shred them, or burn them, if you have the safe means to do so, like a fireplace. As you are discarding your notes, think of it as if you are throwing away all the problems and things that have upset you. Taking them off your plate.

On other pages or another journal, you can also write in the joys and accomplishments of the day. Give gratitude for all that you have and really feel that gratification. Even if things are not going well, there is always someone else that is going through a tougher time than you, so be grateful for everything. Even the negative things are teaching you lessons. You may not always see those lessons right away, but one day you will, and you will appreciate that experience more.

I am usually a patient person, but I also had my impatient moments, and taking care of my ex-husband and dealing with his emotions, taught me a lot of patients. I was able to use that strength to navigate through my life with my ill parent and help my healthier parent deal with the changes in all our lives. Not to mention how patient I had to be going through everything I had experienced with my own health. In my family, of the siblings, I was the calmer one, so it was only natural I thought that the Universe had put me in a position where I was the one helping to care for my ill parent. And all that patience from the past is still helping me to navigate my world as I get older, and I remember to stop and breathe in the air around me. I know now that all is as planned, so there is no reason to fight what I cannot change.

I need to go with the flow of life and let things unfold as they may. Adapting as best as I can to what ever comes my way. Blessing the life lessons that only make me stronger. I know I need to remember to be as patient as I can with myself and those around me that may trigger me and move me out of my comfortable place. But move through life as effortlessly as I can to not cause me any further stress and live with love and gratitude for it all.

Chapter Five

Simple Step Number 4

Learn More About It All

Not everyone likes to research about different symptoms or illnesses one may have and that is okay. Because we have some amazing doctors, specialists, and others in their respective fields that can help us know and understand different ailments.

But I like to go one step further and find out my own information about things. It helps to understand an illness better and know how to cope with situations. Maybe have some questions ready to ask those doctors. I do not want to get home from their office or the hospital and not know how to deal with a medical emergency that has a simple solution and wasn't an emergency after all. Different complications can pop up and you can go crazy trying to find a doctor's office that is open after hours or during holidays, to answer your concerns. I have found in the past that pharmacists can answer some of your questions, so do reach out to them if you cannot get a hold of your doctor.

Having a little more knowledge allows me further understanding of an ailment and how to deal with things like emotional upsets. Do I back off and let the person deal with a situation on their own, or do I get involved and help out. Do I just lend an ear, or remind them of their strengths and amazing qualities, helping them out of feeling hopeless? It's just knowing what type of support one can give.

It also helps me to know if there is anything I need to watch out for such as side effects with medications or even what to expect after those surgeries. I do not know what I do not know, but if I open my eyes and look for guidance on a perplexing problem, I can always be sure to find something that will help me in some way and ultimately, help my loved ones. My research has saved them several times. It just helped me to know if the situation could be handled at home, or if we needed to take further action and involve a professional.

If you accidentally, get a small cut on your finger and the area turns red, most of us know that we may have an infection, so we take steps to heal that. Or if someone has a low fever as opposed to a high fever, again, we know enough to take some type of action. And how many of us research the different symptoms of our young infants before racing to the hospital with them, knowing they need more help than what we can provide for them at home? Especially these days, given what the world is experiencing with the pandemic. So, having some knowledge is good.

When it came to my ex-husband's health issues, even though he was in the care of a doctor, he began to have further emotional upsets, and because I had researched his symptoms, I realized there may have been more to his situation than what was being uncovered. Mostly, because as I mentioned, my ex-husband was a master at disguising his emotions, so he would not tell the doctors everything. Which, of course, did not allow him to have the best treatments to heal, since they didn't know what was fully ailing him.

In doing some of my own research, I knew that if my ex-husband had a change in medications, he could experience mood swings to that medication. Some prescriptions were not strong enough where others were too strong, and I would see his different reactions depending on what he took. That told me we had to look deeper into what he was prescribed by the doctor and maybe tweak the medications. Some medications did not help him at all, and we were back to the old prescriptions until a better one was found.

Those times would be difficult ones for my ex-husband, so I tried to keep him calm and worked at lessening any situations I thought might upset him more. Another thing that helped was changing the subject. It took his mind off worry or concerns about what was bothering him. So, I worked on being as positive as I could and just tried to love him. And that went a long way. He didn't feel alone or abandoned. He knew he had someone there to help him get through whatever he was feeling.

When it comes to medications giving adverse effects remember that some medications can fix one problem but can damage something else. Being aware of what medications can do is important so when you receive those papers from the pharmacist that lists side effects or reactions someone can experience, read them. It can mean the difference between life or death. There may be something in the medication your loved one has an allergy to or may have a reaction that should be given urgent medical attention. Other reactions can be minor and may not be of much concern.

It's a good idea to pick up the phone and call your pharmacy if you are not sure of how to administer the medicine or have any questions. Like should something be taken with food or on an empty stomach? Are there times that are best to take the medications? Your answers can be just a phone call away, and the pharmacists are usually happy to answer them. Better to have the right answers instead of guessing when it comes to medication.

For my ex-husband, his medications were forever having to be adjusted and there were many calls I would make to the pharmacy to ensure one medication did not interfere with the other, or that he was taking them correctly. Depending on what type of medications someone is taking there may also be regular tests one should take like having some blood work done to ensure everything is working fine. This is a good question to ask your doctors as I have heard occasions where you leave the hospital with a prescription but are not given all the details.

Also, check with your pharmacy as they can package medications for you. They are called blister packs which can aid in cutting down confusion on which pills to take and when. There may be a fee attached to the service, so you can inquire, but it is worth doing. It takes a lot of the guesswork out of wondering if you forgot to take some medication and you don't want to be counting them to find out.

When it came to my ex-husband and finding out what was ailing him, the most difficult thing for me was not knowing what was wrong with him when he first began to act strange. He would get emotional and rush out the door of our home, our church, or out of wherever we may have been. It did not matter if we were in deep conversation with others or have a full grocery cart we were pushing. I would be left hanging, trying to explain his disappearance to others. And of course, the hardest to explain to would be the kids.

I knew something was wrong, but we could never get to the bottom of what it was and because my ex-husband had dealt with his symptoms most of his life, everything seemed normal to him. I of course was not versed in mental illness and had a difficult time trying to help my ex-husband understand something was wrong given his constant emotional outbreaks. Something that needed more investigating.

He was very content to continue visiting his doctor and simply having his old prescription renewed, without many adjustments to those prescriptions. It was just routine for him, so any big issues that should have been addressed with the doctor were not.

As time passed my ex-husband had more difficulty in coping with things so he was not aware he was deteriorating, and it was not easy for me to get him to discuss certain symptoms with the doctor. Plus, he was too ashamed to discuss his full symptoms; a weakness for one to not have control over their emotions. Why would he admit to such a thing?

He was fine. At least that was his favorite line to me. But he was not fine. Not at all. How do you help someone when they don't know they need help, and your hands are tied, and you don't know where to turn to get further assistance and support? Sadly, a difficult situation.

But these difficult situations must be figured out or you will not be able to help your loved ones. What worked for us, was to sit with my ex-husband and talk about what was going on and I would be able to discuss some of his actions, trying to show him that they were not normal, and he needed to talk to someone about what was going on with him.

I did, however, always remind him of the great qualities he had as I did not want to only give him the negative things that I saw. So, there was a certain way I had to deal with him. I could not just blurt out the things he did that were strange. That would wound the best of us. I had to deal with him with a delicate nature. A balance of making him aware of what was eating at his emotions and what was making him the great person we all loved. In hopes that this would all bring him back to feeling calm and relaxed, instead of continuing with one of his episodes. Episodes that could last for days.

Again, these are some of the things you can discuss with doctors who are better versed in how to help your loved ones. They will be better able to give you tips on how best to deal with your situation. And given that you know your loved one best, you can tweak things to help them more, using this information.

There were times I would accompany my ex-husband to the doctor's office. Then, we could at least discuss things a little more in-depth, but most times, he would attend on his own, which he was comfortable in doing. Plus, Privacy laws would allow me to only help him so far so I could not attend an appointment if he wanted to go on his own. At the time, he was still able to function well, other than when he would experience one of his mood swings. I feel more help can be given if doctors sit with other family members to discuss the actions of those not well and understand more of what is going on. Since their state of mind is not always clear enough to know what is happening. Then, and only then, do I feel a fuller picture can be painted of what is occurring on a day-to-day basis. Thereby understanding symptoms more and working better with the patient.

Not able to accompany my ex-husband to the doctor's office all the time, I got around some privacy issues, by discussing my own health and concerns, as well as fears, hoping the doctor would pay attention to what I was saying about my ex-husband. It was the only way I knew how to get the information out to help his situation. I had hoped that I would be given tips or more understanding of how to deal with the situation, but sadly, back then, I never was.

All I wanted to do was get back the man I knew before, or at least have him feeling better and able to enjoy life without things haunting him and deteriorating his brain. But as I learned more about it all, I knew that ship had sailed and things had shifted and changed drastically, from the person my ex-husband used to be.

Because he was changing and struggling more with what was going on around him, I wanted to understand what was happening so that I could help him cope better with life events. He would get so overwhelmed with small things that the average person would not. It was just not a normal way to be. I thought that if I understood what was going on with him, I could help my ex-husband through the tough days which in turn would help the entire family.

All I had to go by was what my ex-husband would tell me and what I saw in his actions. However, I learned to look for subtle changes in his behavior that could warn me of an oncoming episode of emotions. I also learned about how the body could get used to different medications and stop working, so I kept an eye open for those changes my ex-husband could experience depending on how long he was on a particular medication. I knew ultimately, the time would come when his doctors would have to make changes to what he was taking.

In the beginning, before I knew what was ailing my ex-husband, I would not monitor him as closely. He would attend his regular doctor's visits, and for the most part, he seemed fine, until his emotions began to change drastically. That was when I did not know how to deal with him. Other than staying calm and patient and helping him work through whatever my ex-husband was going through since we didn't have any outside help coming to our aid other than the family doctor, at the time.

I know I am repeating to stay calm and patient, but it really helped my ex-husband to refocus and feel loved and safe. Which would lessen his emotional explosions. It gave me time to think straight and give him the information that would help him to relax and possibly stop an episode from occurring. Or becoming bigger than it could have, had he been left to deal with things himself and get lost in his emotional turmoil. Had I known more of where to go, I could have helped him further and life would have been better for us all.

Sometimes we were able to work through his difficult episodes together and other times it was better to go to the hospital where there were professionals, we hoped were available to assist him to calm his nerves. But as time passed, I began to see a pattern emerge in his ways. Once I knew what was ailing my ex-husband and had the right diagnosis, it was easier to understand him and help him through whatever emotions he was dealing with at any given time. I also knew when his emotions were too out of control that he would need to visit the emergency department and possibly have a change in medications that I of course could not help with.

Because I knew some of his symptoms, I knew that there were times my ex-husband felt invincible and feel like he did not need his medications and there were many times he would stop taking them. Then, in the place of the man I knew and loved, would emerge this stranger who was belligerent, cruel, cold. So, I feared for his well-being because his moods could come crashing down, his emotions spiraling out of control.

It was difficult at times, but I had to remember to never take what he said or did personally. I knew it was the Bipolar demons making him say and do the things he did. But I also knew I had to make plans to leave the house in a hurry if I had to, given his emotions. That was the case on the day I picked him up and took him to the hospital. I knew he had deteriorated too much for me to no longer feel safe in the house with him and with our young child, and that's when I had to make the difficult decision to leave. His condition was not something I knew how to handle anymore.

Given the ailments my ex-husband had, I also kept an eye on his kids, afraid any one of them could develop similar symptoms to their father, which I was so very grateful was not the case. You see, we learned from the doctors, that if one parent developed an ailment, there was a chance the child of the same sex could also develop the same symptoms at some point in their life.

My fear was so great of any children we had together developing the same ailments as their father, that I only had one child with him. I also felt it was important that once his kids were older, they learn more about what their father was going through so that they understand him and his behaviors. They also had to be aware of the family health history for not only themselves, but for any children, they may have as well in the future. It was always my goal as well, to make sure all my ex-husband's children knew their father loved them, even with his changing ways.

After getting together with one of his older relatives and hearing stories from my ex-husband's childhood, there were things he had done even back then that were out of the ordinary and a little strange. It made me wonder that if my ex-husband's symptoms were understood when he was younger, he may have had an easier time going through life, where he would be better able to cope with things as an adult. As it is Bipolar and other mental health issues, are something that still needs more understanding and there is a lot of red tape one goes through to get help for those that suffer. Yes, our knowledge is improving, but there is still a lot to be done.

If someone experiences a mental disposition and they are lucky enough to not get caught up in the red tape of bureaucratic chaos, they may actually get help through the hospitals and the government bodies governing these departments. But if they are unlucky enough to not go through the correct hoops, they could spend their lives going in and out of doctor's offices that do not know how to fully help them, in and out of institutions that quickly assess them and let them back out into a world, they cannot cope with and possibly on the streets, spending the rest of their lives, still trying to figure out what is wrong with them.

Who helps those people find their way or function in society, in life? It can be maddening, stressful, and drive the entire family to help or give up, broken, at some point and let the person fend for themselves, not realizing there is a medical condition that is letting them act out.

When my ex-husband was released the following day without contacting me, left me demoralized in a health system we depend on. No one contacted me to discuss how to best help him, what to watch out for or do if this happened again, or even transition from what he was presently experiencing. He was left to his own accord, ready to fall to pieces all alone. I know, no system is perfect, but I had dropped him off as he heard voices in his head the day before. He was still fragile the following day, regardless of whatever medications they may have given him to calm down. I thought, even more reason to contact his family to take care of him. He was still having suicidal thoughts and I feared still a danger to himself and others.

They never gave him a regiment to follow, maybe putting him on some program that would help to stabilize his moods or find a psychiatrist he could stick to when he needed more assistance. They never told me what his condition might be once he was out of the hospital and what to look out for so I could keep helping him. They just released him to his responsibility when he still could not function well. Those are the souls lost in a bureaucratic system and I feel it is up to us their families that should advocate for them when we can. My heart hurts for those people that do not have much family to count on or families who have given up on their strange ways and left their loved ones to fend for themselves.

When it came to my ill parent's health and making sure I knew the information I needed to know, to give the best care to them I also tried to learn as much as I could. Not only through researching the ailments, but by asking many questions. I had a lot of concerns. I took mental notes, writing some things down, as I observed the doctors and nurses so that I would not forget things later since it was a crazy and exhausting time. You may not need to do this in your situation, but we had many things we had to be aware of, so I didn't want to forget anything important that could become detrimental to my parent's health.

As I watched the nurses, therapists, and PSW's care for my parent, it helped me to know what I needed to do once we got my parent at home. This not only reduced my stress level since I had a life, I had to take care of, but it reduced the stress for both my parents. They were going through enough. The last thing I wanted was to have any one of them be concerned about the quality of care at home.

Not to mention that I would never have forgiven myself if something happened to my ill parent that could have been avoided. So, I had better know my stuff inside out. And keep in mind, taking someone home and having to care for them is a big job, and I say often, it is not for everyone, so don't look back at what you have done or not done or are doing now and blame yourself for not caring for your loved ones enough, because everything you do is enough and makes a difference. And if that also means you stepping back and letting others do the big jobs while you do the smaller ones, then that's ok too.

The hospital informed us about some of the things we needed to be aware of so that my parent had a safe environment. But it was up to us to inform others that came to help about my parent's health issues. Some of the PSW's were not entirely up to speed on their condition so it was exhausting to continue to repeat it with every new worker that came in, but it had to be done. I would have hated to see what would have happened if it had been just both my parents at home with the helpers coming because my healthier parent could not speak English well and would not remember all the finer details that the workers needed to know.

So, if you are ever in a position where you have outside caregivers, be sure to keep them up to date on any changing issues and any new workers that come are knowledgeable about your loved one's situation. Because things can change quickly. This is where it's a good idea to put a book in the main area of where the action happens so that everyone can communicate what the needs for the day are should you not be present. I would also suggest you call when the caregiver is supposed to show up at the home if you are not there because we have run into situations where I had to call to find out where the PSW was since it would be well into the half-hour mark, and no one would be there. Nor would we get a call to find out if the person was late, or even coming at all. On one occasion, the receptionist answering my call at the business office insisted the worker was behind the door, yet there was no one there. only to find out they were at the incorrect address and ready to leave.

We have run into situations where the PSW's would forget some of the important information they needed to know about my parent's care and only because I was there would I be able to correct something. My ill parent had to have any liquids at a certain consistency and should not be given a straw to drink with as it could cause harm and lead to other major problems. One day, I had prepared water with the correct consistency for my ill parent to drink, but my healthier parent moved it behind another bottle on the table. The PSW did not see it and innocently went to our supplies to get another water bottle. Then asked my healthier parent for a straw, which again, innocently they gave them, thinking it was for the PSW's own drink. My healthier parent and I were off doing other chores, and I happened to walk into the kitchen just as the lady was about to give the bottle to my parent to drink.

At the time, my parent still did not have the strength to hold the bottle, which the worker had forgotten that I had mentioned. But that was not what I was worried about. The water had not been thickened as well as she was giving my parent the straw to drink with. At least I was able to stop her before she continued.

Because foods also had to be pureed and a specific texture I researched how to best do this so that my parent enjoyed what they were eating. Mouthfuls could not be given too fast, and because we had new and changing PSW's we had to make sure they each knew what to do. This also included learning how to use the equipment that would move my parent from one place to another.

We were made aware that the therapist that had taught us how to best use the equipment, would also come back, to show the PSW's that came to help as well as the different therapy that could be done by them. This was so relieving to know because at least we were able to make sure the people that came to the house were educated about our situation. Again, this relieved a lot of stress and worry for us all. I made sure each family member that came and was willing to learn how to use the equipment was also present because we of course did not want any accidents.

So, reach out to the company that you are working with to find out if they offer this service as well. At least you can ensure that your loved one is taken care of and they will help you to look after your loved one properly. Also reach out to your government agencies, because at least here in Ontario, there are other services that they can assist with, from various types of therapists and specialists, coming to help in aiding your loved ones to, nurses that can come to help with various things too. There are also services for doctors and dentists, that will come to the house, but those would most likely require a fee. Some family doctors will make house calls, and we were very grateful to my parent's doctor, who did indeed come periodically to make house visits.

I also found out that at the time, if we needed to call Emergency Services the payment for their trip to the hospital would be paid for by the government services that we were connected with, that assisted seniors. This was helpful to know because my parents were able to be reimbursed for those trips and I knew that the next time we had a hospital trip, I would tell the person at the front desk, and usually, they would manage the paperwork from their end. Each situation is different of course as are the rules and regulations for each province, city, state, or town, so you can inquire if this is covered for you.

Some of the equipment that is needed to care for your loved ones, like wheelchairs, walkers, or canes, are also covered by our government services, at least a portion of the payments are. Even if you need stairlifts and you are having financial trouble to afford this, reach out to your social workers and government services, as there are charities that may be able to assist if you qualify.

Find out also what the timeframes are for replacing parts on wheelchairs as opposed to replacing the entire chair. At present, we can change the parts every two years, and the entire chair or walking apparatus is every five years, but then again, all that can change, given any government changes.

Also, find out what type of transit is available and the paperwork you need to get filled out to be able to transport your loved one back and forth. Find out, how many trips you are allowed to miss if you must cancel and the advanced times you need to give them. You can usually check on their websites or call the transport companies to find out if your trip is still on time.

I remember calling for a dentist appointment for my ill parent and hanging up after choosing a suitable date. I called right back moments later, wondering if the wheelchair would fit not only through the office doors, as we had already discussed but into their examination room with the dentist chair and the other equipment around. I had never been to that office, so I did not know the setup.

Sure enough, my extra questioning led me back to measure my parent's wheel size on the wheelchair a few times, to ensure we would be okay. It turned out that we had to either, find another dentist to go to that would accommodate wheelchair access or have our family members accompany us to help lift my ill parent out of the wheelchair and into the doctor's chair. Had I not been so inquisitive, we would have gone through the entire trip of getting my ill parent to the appointment, only to have to turn back around and go home. And believe me, when you are dealing with certain ailments, the last thing you want to do is wait around for hours until your transportation gets to you. It's very uncomfortable when someone is not well and just wants to get home into bed. We had a few long days, with my parent, getting them to various appointments and some days were traumatic for them. So, you certainly want to make sure the trips are made as comfortable as you can, which is difficult to control many times of course.

Hospitals are also great to get a hold of for certain appointments because they will be more wheelchair accessible and may be able to direct you to other places to assist you. Some government programs have places that you can take your loved ones to spend the day there. An outing of sorts. In that way, they are not left at home to be bored but can get out and socialize with others. It is good for you to get out there too.

Do your research and learn as much about the ailments that are hindering your loved ones as well as the various services available to you. The more you learn, the happier you and your loved ones will be, making life a little easier to breathe. Learn as much as you can about what you can do to help because you may be dealing with this situation for a while. You may find there are many layers to the bureaucratic system that seems to get more confusing as time passes but if you are aware of how to navigate it, you will be further ahead than behind. Talk to the doctors and get involved as much as they will allow you to with your loved one's situation. Find out what avenues you have as a family member, friend or other, that are available to you to assist your loved ones.

Some people may have trouble getting help for those suffering from a mental illness because their loved ones do not think there is anything wrong with them and have the right to refuse any help. Or my not know how to best navigate the system. They may not speak English well or be new to the country and not know where to go to find someone that speaks their language or where to go for help. Some people may not have the use of computers or know how to use them so again, they may be closed off from finding what they need. Our government here in Ontario has many places you can reach out to for help and I'm sure so do many other provinces, cities, or states. So, if you are aware of anyone in this position, give them a helping hand if you can.

In more severe cases, if your loved one is not feeling well and does not acknowledge they are ill, you may need to get legal papers to insist they get the medical attention that can stabilize their emotions. If you live in Ontario and are struggling to get your loved one help, research what Form 1, or Form 2 is and if it will help you to get your loved ones in some psychiatric facilities that can assist with their healing. Form 1 is an application filled out by the physician that is monitoring a patient to have them undergo a psychiatric assessment to determine whether the person needs to be admitted for further care in a psychiatric facility. This can be involuntary or voluntary. Then they can assess if the person is well enough to be discharged.

Form 2 is an "Order for Examination," under the Mental Health Act of Ontario, and it is signed by the Justice of the Peace. It is an order for an assessment by a doctor. Form 2 is based on sworn statements from a family member or someone who closely knows your loved one who can explain what is going on with their health and that they may require assistance for their mental well-being.

So, write down what goes on with your loved ones over time, so that you have a record of everything. If you need to go back further in time to explain different events that your loved one has gone through, related to the mental illness, you will have it handy, instead of recalling from your memory. If you have other doctors available that have worked with your loved one and they have their own evaluations, get them to add to the story. It will paint a picture for the doctors to help evaluate your loved one at that time and help them how they can. I didn't know so much of this back then with my ex-husband, so it was like we were starting all over again, every time he would go to the hospital.

If your loved one can function well on their own for the most part, and they are fine to work with the doctors they have in place, I would say to still keep an eye on them in case their symptoms change and become worse. Make sure they take their medications for example and stick to the program that may be laid out for them. That way they can be stable and live a comfortable life, not to mention not give you or other family members, further stress.

Learning more about the various ailments also gives you peace of mind. You become aware of what to look out for and know how to better handle changing moods and situations. It also makes you aware of just how bad a situation can get and help you stop that in its tracks. This will remove extra stresses from not only your life, but everyone involved and maybe even gives you time to breathe before the next ailment hits.

With my ill parent, we learned as much as we could about their illness and how to make them comfortable. We were able to plan, knowing where things could take us. Given what we knew, we could detect signs of other ailments that we knew could occur, so we would keep an eye open for those too. I also kept a journal on their symptoms so that if a doctor asked us a question about changing symptoms, I was able to answer it right away, helping my loved one. It also helped to write things down, because you may remember the incident at that moment, but months down the road, you may not, given the many other things you must remember. Some information can be important, and you don't want to miss it.

Learning about the changing ailments of someone is an ongoing process and believe me, there were days with my ex-husband and my parent, where I felt like a doctor as I researched information when I did not get the answers from the professionals or wanted a second opinion. It just kept me aware of things and I could have an intelligent conversation with the doctors about what was going on with my loved ones and kept the doctors accountable too. Not to say they did not know what they were doing, because we had great doctors, but there may be some bit of information you provide that can help in understanding an ailment and knowing more makes you aware of other illnesses that could be creeping up.

The more I spoke to others who were experiencing a similar situation, the more I learned and the more I was able to help my loved one and other people I met.

So, learn all you can to help with any surprises and give you a chance to plan for what comes next. You will thank yourself for staying one step ahead of the game.

Chapter Six

Simple Step Number 5

Rest When You Can

I say it all the time. Rest when you can. We get so busy caring for our loved ones, we forget to care for ourselves. With my ex-husband, I was juggling a lot of his emotional issues, along with everything else that comes with raising a family and just life in general. By the end of the day, I was exhausted. But I kept on going, never thinking to take a break from the busy workday, before getting into the second shift of the evening routines.

I could have left a chore for another day when maybe things would not be so busy, but I didn't. I could have folded laundry later or vacuumed another time, but I didn't do that either. It was like I had to prove to myself, my ex-husband, the Universe, somebody, that I could handle everything thrown at me and get everything on my list done. Because, well, because wasn't that what we were supposed to do? Make sure our household ran smoothly, so when someone looked for a particular shirt, it was washed. If we needed more dishes, they were available and not sitting in the dishwasher or the sink. My ex-husband was amazing and did help with chores, but most things were left for me. Especially, after he was experiencing more emotional upsets which I understood.

Most evenings I was ready for bed by nine pm. As hard as I tried to keep my eyes open I could not. I was usually up for about five in the morning to get ready for work and bring our young child to daycare. After work, it was me that had to rush back to pick up our child, take them along to get groceries, and run whatever other errands were needed. Of course, once I got home, there was the cooking and cleaning up, and since my child responded better with me putting them to bed, it was usually my job. Then, I would get back to whatever other chores may be left for the night.

This is not much different than what other families do on most days, I know, but because I was getting up so early and handling so much myself, the added stress of looking after my ex-husband's emotional needs was draining me. It would be a night spent at the hospital or up through the night talking and trying to calm down his emotions, then back up before the sun rose again to begin my day. I was falling asleep while driving to work in the morning and I was getting sicker myself but did not see the signs.

Most of us keep going and when the weekend comes, and work is over, we can take that downtime, and this was something I did not take advantage of. I know many people that do not either because let's face it, there is always something else to do. We forget that we need to take the time to rest and be with ourselves or our loved ones, doing things we enjoy.

I am a very light sleeper, and I don't know how many times, I would get up through the night, hearing the television on and I knew my ex-husband had fallen asleep in front of it. There were other health issues to worry about, so I could not even leave him there for the night, not to mention, that he would be pretty sore from sleeping on the couch, in the morning had I done that. As comfortable as it was.

I was young then, and of course, I would not notice how tired I would be until it started to catch up to me as time passed. It took a lot to bring me down, and I was the type that only needed a small nap, then I was back up and energized again. But, as I mentioned, I was getting different signs and did not pay attention to my health. Even when I woke up one day, and could not straighten out my back, did I realized I was pushing my body too hard.

I was cutting the grass in the summer and had my little garden and flowers I enjoyed tending to. The winters found me shoveling snow and doing so much more throughout the year. I was strong from always working out in the past, so I never thought anything of the things I had to do. I just did them. Even the massage therapist that I went to that day when I was unable to straighten up, told me to go home after the session and take an Epson bath and relax. I had no time to relax.

I never realized until my parent fell ill, and I was so stressed out, that I should have changed things long ago to give me some breathing room. Maybe make things easier so that I did have the time to rest when my body called for it. Like when I felt those pins and needles in my back or the drowsiness while driving. I should have stopped. Instead, I just kept piling on the stress and lack of sleep, and only succeeded in adding more to my plate as time went on. I never took time to enjoy life around me either. My ex-husband needed caring, my child needed me, and I made sure I was always there for them. The house needed my attention and so did my family and friends.

Take note of how you part your time throughout the day and how many times you actually, take the time to rest. When you are at work, your employer is entitled to give you a break several times throughout the day. Why is it that we do not give ourselves that same resting period? We have to remember that at times we may have the energy to continue onward, but we may pay for it in exhaustion or pain later, so we have to pace ourselves.

When I think of all the things I did through these years, it is no wonder I ended up having health issues as I got older. It only takes changing a few things in your day to stop and rest your body and your mind. We must not let others govern our bodies because they do not know what we need. Nor what you have been through or going through. I remember feeling guilty many times going down to rest when I was caring for my ill parent. There was just so much to do and if I did not get to something, my other parent would do it and keep on going as well. I could not have that.

But then again, I was already experiencing my health crisis and could only do so much before I would shut down and I would fight back tears and keep going knowing both my parents needed whatever strength I could muster. Nobody knew how much pain I was really in. When I would finally get a moment to rest which did not happen often, I would feel guilty, thinking others thought I was not doing enough.

This is why I say, do not let others tell you when you need to stop and rest or push you into doing more than you can. No matter what you are doing. Take the breather your body needs and do not let guilt stop you from taking that rest. I, unfortunately, learned the hard way and hope that by reading my stories you will come to understand that we are so important as well, yet we never blink an eye to look after our ailments the way we would if it was a loved one.

Continuing to care for my ill parent and being up round the clock with them was taking its toll on my health which kept declining. But again, I never stopped. I just kept going. I thought I was strong and could take a lot. So, I tried to do as much as I could to remove stress, from my other parent so they did not get overwhelmed or overworked as they too tried to help and were burning out. They were not healthy and not young anymore.

What I should have done was taken that step back and not let others dictate my day, which was what I was allowing them to do. When I needed to rest, I should have taken it. When I was in pain, I should have stopped. As the daughter living with my parents, I wanted to look after them as they had done for me growing up. Yet, how many parents employ nannies or have daycare arrangements, maybe get a babysitter to help them out, or for a night out on the town to keep their sanity? How many grandparents spend time with their grandkids, while the parents take some time alone? Or even just to catch up on some much-needed sleep? Yet, when we are caregivers, we don't reach out that hand for help. Sometimes even within our own families.

There were days my head would spin, and I was afraid to even go driving, because I knew I was not sleeping enough or resting enough, not to mention I had this fear of leaving my parents alone. If anything happened to my healthier parent, who was also not resting and stressed, beyond capacity, the ill one, of course, was not capable of assisting. If anything happened to my ill parent, the healthier parent could get easily confused and not think of going to the phone to dial for help right away. I had placed a big note on the refrigerator door with the words, 'Emergency – 911', in big red letters as well as had added all the children and grandchildren's names on the page. I had also placed a big note over the wall, where the main telephone was so that anyone coming into the house could easily identify the important family numbers to dial in case of emergencies.

Talk about caregiver burnout. I was not sleeping well, was not very hungry and as much as I was a social butterfly, I did not care to go and meet up with friends or do the things I used to love doing before. I was too tired. Plus, we were so busy with full days of round-the-clock caregiving. My entire life had been caring for my ex-husband, followed closely by caring for my ill parent and making sure the other one did not fall prey to any other major illnesses or get themselves into mischief because they too did not know when to stop nor did they understand they were not young anymore. If they fell ill or hurt themselves, I knew I would be in bigger trouble.

Some days, I tried to rest when my ill parent would so that I could catch up on my sleep, but that would not last long. My other parent would be off doing something else, pushing themselves as I was doing and I, of course, would join them so that they would not have to do whatever chore they found to keep them busy, alone. And yes, they always found something new to keep them occupied. Often, I would have to pull them away from something and let them rest. This is something that must be done sometimes for you and those caring for others. Because often we don't know when to stop as you can see from my stories.

When there is a life change, especially the kind we were experiencing with my parent, it is prudent to change the way you spend your time, because other things may take priority. Being European, my parents used to do many things the old way, but instead of the healthier parent adopting new ways suggested by the family or by our government health providers, they continued to spend their day adding these chores to an already crazy, busy day and they would stress themselves out trying to fit everything in.

The homemade breadcrumbs had to be made from the many pieces of leftover bread, to dry out in the oven, instead of buying a container of crumbs at the store. In the summer, there were the tomatoes from the garden that had to be made into sauce, doing it the old-fashioned way, using a food mill that you had to turn and turn and turn until the tomatoes were squished and made into sauce. Jam from the fruit trees had to be made and on and on it went well into Christmas and into the next year.

There were times I would find my healthier parent with one leg outside a window on the top floor of the house, as they tried to clean the inside and outside windows in the spring or climb a rickety ladder that we tried many times to throw away, only to find it back in its spot. We had an old table and chair set from when I was a little girl, and my healthier parent would climb this chair constantly to clean the bathroom mirrors or other higher objects. Granted the chair was a sturdy one, made from steel, and believe it or not, it is still kicking around today, but it was old, and all it would take would be one dizzy spell or a different movement from my parent and down they could go if they were not careful.

So, along with my health issues and raising my kid on my own and wanting to give them the time they needed as well, I had my ill parent to tend to and had my hands full, watching the other parent who did not make life any easier. They thought nothing of sneaking outside in the middle of a snowstorm in the early morning hours. I mean like, at four in the morning, to clear the snow off with my old snowblower when they could barely move the machine themselves and their health was of great concern. Not to mention they were well into their 80's and frail. We had a snow removal service and my kid who was older now, was there to help, but my parent would be too impatient to wait for either one. So, as much as I did not want to, knowing we could use the machine in the future, I sold it to remove that obstacle.

I tried to keep them out of trouble by not getting sprayed by skunks in the back yard as they chased them away or injure themselves, during a major windstorm as they tried to hold up the backyard fence that strong winds were blowing over and almost blowing them over in the process. Thank goodness for my kid who heard me yelling and ran outside just in time to move their grandparent out of the way of a flying beam that could have hurt them both. You can imagine how upsetting this can be to put someone else in peril. As if we did not have our hands full already. As you can see, caring for someone is not always just the person who is not well, but there are entire dynamics that go along with the job.

At times I would walk around the house, wondering where my healthier parent was and what they were up to now, only to hear my ill parent screaming as they would see their spouse leaning a one-sided ladder on the fruit trees in the yard, pruning them and reaching out, the ladder moving precariously back and forth on the thin tree trunk. Like a daredevil, they would tease us and rock the ladder that much more, wanting to show us how secure they were, which of course, was not the case. I would be in the middle of feeding my ill parent and would have to stop to try and get my healthier parent in the house which was no easy task.

It was difficult to get the proper rest in the environment I was in. I was in the middle of writing a kid's book, 'Ghost Detective The Magic Ruby', which is sold now on Amazon, and would stay up to get some writing done. I had to tend to my ill parent anyway so I figured I may as well just keep writing until I was really, sleepy. I think my writing had helped me to unwind. It was my therapy. Then, just as I would get ready for bed, I would have to get back up to tend to my ill parent again.

Several times a week I would wake up at six in the morning, to the sounds of the old washing machine as it squealed and screeched and banged the clothes around as it washed them. Where I was up most of the night, my healthier parent would get to bed with my other parent, so they would be wide awake and beginning chores way too early for anyone in the house. I knew they were up because they could not rest either and their mind was buzzing a hundred miles a minute of all the things to get done during the week, not to mention to keep their mind busy. The only problem with beginning the washing machine so early was that it would wake my ill parent up and it would throw their sleep off for the day, not to mention that then we would all be up. Including my kid who had to attend school and could not get back to sleep.

I knew I had to put a stop to this madness, but it was difficult to get my healthier parent to slow down and maybe rest more, even during the day, when my ill parent would nap. They did take some time to rest here and there but felt guilty and would keep moving. So, it did not always work, but at least when we did rest, it helped to re-energize us somewhat.

It took a few years for me to step away at times and leave my healthier parent to do the extra things they were not ready to give up or change as long as they were safe. I understood they needed to keep busy, but I was going crazy juggling my time between both parents and my own family. As well as my health hindering me with things. The stress did not help. I had to let some things go or I wasn't going to be around to help anyone.

I had to come to terms with letting go and allow my healthier parent to do what they needed to and function the way things felt right to them. If my healthier parent wanted to continue to work themselves to death, then I had to let them do it and not follow them in the process. That would be their journey, not mine. The last thing I wanted was to get to the point where I could no longer look after my parents and put them in a nursing home or not be around for my kid. As hard as I tried to do it all, in the end, I just could not anymore, health issues changed for all of us, and the family had to make other arrangements to find outside care for my parents. That guilt alone was a big blow to me, and it took a while to bounce back from that. But I also knew that I had done all I could.

I have spoken to other caregivers, and I find the same story. We work ourselves to the bone, making sure our loved ones are looked after but we do not look after ourselves. There are the ill person's needs to look after which could be a lot on its own, depending on the ailment, the equipment you may have to use, heavy lifting may need to be done. Then there are other family members, emotional turmoil to deal with, cooking, cleaning, more chores, depending on what the ailment is, and not enough time in the day to take care of you and everything else.

This is why I say to rest when you can. If it is ten minutes, take it, because you may not get that time again during the day and those ten minutes can make a difference. Sometimes we may have to just slow down and let some of the chores go for a few days longer. Maybe it is not cleaning the entire home from top to bottom, as was our customary thing to do, every week. We had no pets, and we kept the place spotless. Some of the rooms that were not lived in any longer, since my siblings had long moved out, could have been cleaned, for example, every other week. If the laundry can be left an extra day, leave it, and go down to rest that weary head. Sometimes, resting can also be doing something that calms you. It can be a bath or doing a hobby that relaxes you, such as I was doing with my writing. Sitting down for a coffee or tea. Sometimes it could also just be staring into space, sitting down with that favorite drink of yours.

After going through what I did when I was with my ex-husband and then taking care of my ill parent, I wish to stress to you please STOP and rest when you can. Take a nap when the person you are caring for does or go to bed early. Call on help from others and delegate what you can so you have a chance to recharge your batteries. Do not feel guilty because you have chores piling up and you are resting. The chores can wait. Your health needs you first. Find relief however you can and take care of yourself AND your loved ones.

Rest so you can be at your best. Rest so you can be there for everyone else that loves you too. Listen to your body and give it the time it needs now. Not tomorrow or another day when you have already begun to fall apart and cannot change the damage you may have caused to yourself.

Chapter Seven

Simple Step Number 6

Communication

Communication is always important to keep everybody informed about what is going on around them. I feel this is especially so when you have someone with a mental disposition and coping with a lot of things. There may be events they don't recall or just plain forget about getting something done. It's also important when you are caring for someone that cannot express themselves well. It is difficult on an average day for anyone. Things as simple as, who is picking up the kids tonight, or as difficult as someone complaining of chest pains, and you don't understand how bad they are feeling.

How many times have you waited for someone at one place when they were waiting somewhere else because the signals got crossed? Or gave someone more medication than they should have had, or for that matter, the wrong one? Only because someone thought the first dose was not administered. Or the medicine looked like another? We have experienced this with my elderly parents and nurses. Let me tell you, we all had our hearts skip a few beats, waiting through the day as one parent was monitored, hoping there would be no repercussions.

Communicating with doctors about symptoms and what is going on is also very important. Your doctor is not going to know what one is feeling or experiencing unless you discuss things, so they may have a harder time trying to diagnose your loved ones. This is why I mentioned before to make sure and get your files from previous doctors over to any new doctors, so they can get a picture of what has been going on and maybe better piece together how they can help going forward. As well as hold on to previous notes you may have that can also help the doctors understand an ailment.

Communicating includes listening and talking with someone, especially if you see that your loved one is not happy one day over another. They could quietly be communicating something to you by just their body language. So be prepared to have a dialogue about what they are really trying to tell you if you see their demeanor change or they are easily upset or won't talk to you. Their tone of voice may change, or their facial expression may tell you something is bothering them. Most of you will know when someone you love is not themselves or upset. Instead of just shrugging it off, check in with them and have a chat. There can be some interesting information uncovered and can bring relationships closer building a special bond. Plus, it could make a difference for your loved one and possibly stopping an emotional upset.

I usually could tell by the look on my ex-husband's face if he was upset or something had changed with his moods. I would stop and take the time to listen to his needs or concerns and that way we could deal with anything that was bothering him, then and there. Not to mention that if he did not get things off his chest, it would stay bottled up inside of him and would make things worse.

Communicating allows for plans to work a little smoother and it helps everyone to stay on track of any changes in appointments or events. It is especially important when it comes to changes in medications or changing health and relaying that information to different caregivers and even to your doctors who are also involved in your loved one's care.

Among many other reasons, when you do not communicate clearly and pay attention, it can lead to frustrations, anger, and confusion. For example, if someone tells you to turn left, do they mean your left or theirs, which plan of action should be followed over another. I got left in the city, one night by my ex-husband when I was very pregnant. We lived more than an hour away by car and the busses and trains were no longer running to my destination for the night. We had just bought our first house and were supposed to sign papers at the lawyer's office. My ex-husband and I were supposed to meet there. To this day, I do not know where my ex-husband had parked or what he had done to find me. Let alone how he figured I would get home that evening. As you can see, it is still a sore subject, so many years later, and that is precisely why communicating information and being as clear as one can is important.

The lawyer said my ex-husband had come upstairs, signed the papers, and left. I must have arrived after him because we did not cross paths. I waited in the office for a few hours and went downstairs to look for him several times. But again, it was a big place, and he could have been anywhere. I continued to call his cell phone, but nobody picked it up.

My ex-husband told me later he had left the phone at home that day. Finally, the lawyer had to lock up and so I made my way down the elevator from the top floors and wondered how I was going to get home. It would be a cab, but I had to find one that would go the distance to where I lived, and even if I were lucky enough to find one, it would cost a pretty penny. I finally called family and after two hours of transferring a few busses, to get me to a certain point, a family member met me and took me the rest of the way home, which I was so very grateful for.

It was a very long night. My ex-husband was at home, happily having his dinner, relaxed, and feeling great. I on the other hand was frazzled, very tired from the trip, and embarrassed at having to call my family while my ex-husband sat at home. It was strange to see his nonchalant attitude when he was usually so loving and caring. I had already experienced some of his strange behaviors by then, but nothing to the extent of how uncaring he had been that night for my welfare. I had racked my brain trying to figure out what had triggered this attitude of his. I did not yet know his diagnosis.

Where I should have discussed the matter with my ex-husband that evening, so that a similar experience would not occur, I did not. I felt it would not have mattered either way, since my ex-husband did not always think things through. But it had upset me that he would not think of my wellbeing and that of his unborn child, and so there it was, stress adding to what I was already beginning to feel in our new marriage when all I had to do was to communicate with my ex-husband and of course, hope that he would communicate back. And even if he would not, at least I would know that I tried to understand and to work this situation out.

My ex-husband was always forgetting things and there were many doctor appointments missed. Some of those appointments were expensive and most of them you had to pay even if you did not show up. Some of the appointments were important ones. At times, my ex-husband could have cared less about missing them, other times he would blame himself for forgetting about them which could easily bring him on a downward spiral. It just depended on his moods. To make things easier and hopefully avoid any further nights, like the one at the lawyers, I started writing things down in a big calendar for the family. My ex-husband got used to checking it every day and it helped to keep him on track with appointments and events.

We even went one step further as new technology was beginning to be unveiled. There was a gadget that looked like a horizontal phone that you could push up the top to find a keyboard underneath and input your appointments and meetings, instead of carrying pieces of paper everywhere with your notes. At least that was what I did. The calendar helped my ex-husband to stay on track at times.

There were times when my ex-husband would visit a doctor and his medication would be changed and I could see his moods beginning to shift. So, I would always be asking him if he had taken his medications the way they had been prescribed to him.

As the years passed, I noticed the family benefitted from having family meetings, where everyone was able to talk things out instead of holding any anger or things that would upset them inside. The important rule here was that I made it a safe place to talk. Not a place where one can bash the other, name-call, or belittle. There was no anger or raising voices. No, 'I told you so', or 'parent knows best'. It was respecting everyone and what they were saying or felt. I did these family gatherings often with my kid and my step-kids as well, and we also talked between my ex-husband and myself, so we too could air out anything we wanted to discuss as a couple. I know, I needed to have done this the night I was left at the lawyers. Sadly, I had not adopted this idea at the time.

Airing things out did help the family to feel comfortable and they were able to express their needs, fears, or concerns and it kept everyone happy. How often have you seen poor communication leading some couples or other family members to be upset with each other over the smallest things? Yet nobody takes the time to explain or clear up a situation. In some cases, ego gets in the way and either party feels the other should make the first move, yet again, nobody does. It can be as simple as one person interpreting the words of another incorrectly.

In some families or even cultures, children are often ignored or silenced and not able to voice their opinions. I mean, how many problems can a young person have? They certainly can't have as many as the adults, right? Wrong. They may be little and may not have had as many years to navigate this world, but they have their own things to deal with. Relationships with parents, siblings, other family members, school, teachers, friends, and so much more. And they have to understand it all given the few years they have been on this earth.

Unable to express themselves, they can feel unloved and disconnected from the family unit. They may feel all alone or like their needs are not being met. Feeling like they are not important can lead to behavior problems. If they can express themselves, at least they have a chance to not only have the stage to air out their concerns, but they feel a part of the family. For me, I made it a point to tell my kid often, I loved them, and being a hugger, I gave lots of those out.

When you are spending so much time caring for someone it is easy to forget to give others in your circle some attention and at times you may be struggling to even find the time to give them. Because we had so much emotional turmoil going on in our household, I felt it especially important to carve out some of that precious time and keep the communication lines open between everyone.

My hope was that we would all understand each other better thereby elevating some of the stress in the family. It helped to calm some fears and understand what ailments others were going through, especially on my ex-husband's down days. Unfortunately, as time passed, and he began to have more emotional episodes, it became harder to communicate with him and that was when it felt like he was just a boarder in the house, coming and going without much communication. As difficult as those days were, I continued to try and reach out to him as much as I could.

When it came to caring for my ill parent, communication was very important. There were two of us looking after them, so we had to make sure we did not overlap on what needed to be done. Especially, when it came to giving medications. That was one of my many chores. Pills had to be crushed and administered with some other food to go down easily. We had to make sure the right medication was given at the right times and if any other pains would arise, we had to make sure we understood what it was so that we could give the right medication, or get a doctor involved to find out what was ailing them.

We also had part-time caregivers, so they had to know what was going on, especially when it came to medications. The PSW's that came in also had to know the situation and they changed often, so again, I was forever repeating myself, making sure they knew what needed to be done.

I wrote down all the information I thought would help the other caregivers look after my ill parent, because there would, of course, be times I would not be there. I would update that information when needed. Then I put a notepad in the kitchen, where most of the action happened, and all the caregivers could communicate with each other or with us as to what was happening to my parent or any other concerns.

Communication between siblings so everyone knew what was going on was also important to calm everyone's nerves. Especially, when it came to the trips to the hospital. If either one of my parents were not well the other siblings knew what was going on. In that way, if there were any trips to the emergency room or the doctor's office, everyone knew how to help them.

I found communicating information was very important as well when we were in the hospital with my ill parent. We had to make sure we clearly, relayed different symptoms my parent may have had to the staff and keep them up to date on any changes so that things would not become a bigger issue.

I mentioned earlier that listening was also important as are many other ways of communicating. There were many days when my ill parent was trying to tell us something they could not find the words to, given their state of mind. It could be something simple like raising their head on the bed or more serious like certain pains that were starting and had to be addressed immediately.

I would understand one thing and my healthier parent another. But I listened and watched for other signs, like where they were pointing too, or where their eyes would look, and I would be able to put things together. From then on, I understood their new way of trying to tell us a specific thing. It cut back on everybody's stress.

One of the therapists that came to help us even suggested printing out pictures of things that my ill parent could point to if they wanted to tell us something and could not find those words. Like the fact that they wanted some water or strawberries. Remember, this was a new way of living for my ill parent, so many things were going to change for everybody. It was challenging, but we learned quickly how to keep them as comfortable as we could.

I also had that big Emergency List for my healthier parent as I mentioned before, and for the caregivers to have quick access to the numbers. Sure, they had all our information in their cell phones, but my healthier parent was not tech-savvy, and I knew if anybody needed a number quickly, they knew where to find it. There was no scrolling through their phones, trying to find our numbers. Especially, with the ever-changing PSW's or caregivers.

As I mentioned earlier, communication back and forth is so very important to understand where someone is coming from, understand their fears, their needs, and yours as well. It's a two-way street, and communication does not have to stop with your immediate family. If you feel you need to let off some steam by way of talking to someone else that can help you through what you are experiencing as a caregiver, do it. If, of course, they are someone that you trust with your information, and can be helpful, instead of making things worse.

Communication I feel is so very important to gain trust and improve relationships that may have otherwise ended. It reduces misunderstandings, conflicts, and a lot of stress. When you are caregiving and more than one person is looking after someone as we were, it is easy to mix up information if you are not careful. As I mentioned before, maybe someone already administered medications, so you do not want to do it again. Maybe you thought someone did the laundry when they did not and now you are looking for clean clothes to put on your loved one. An appointment got missed because someone forgot to change the dates and was not available. This all leads to anger and blaming everybody else when all you have to do is just talk.

Much of our world revolves around communications, and many wars have started from lack of it. Many have ended because of it. So do not discount the power of communications when it comes to your household and looking after those you love. Their life can depend on it.

So, keep the door open and exchange information back and forth. Don't leave it up to the other person. Take the initiative. You may be glad you did.

Chapter Eight

Simple Step Number 7

Stay Organized

Just like good communication, staying organized is important as well. You may have a bunch of chores to do, but you didn't give yourself the time to do them yesterday. You were so busy with your caregiving role, so now you have yesterday's chores and today's things to do too. This is when you begin to get stressed. Will you have the time today? And if not, when will they get done? You know they are a priority. Maybe it's laundry that needs to get washed because otherwise, you will not have any clean clothes for your loved one who is not well, so what do you do?

To top it off, because you are playing catch up with yesterday and today's chores, you don't take the time to eat right, because, well, there just wasn't time. So, then you get to sleep, but your mind is thinking about all the things you must do, so you may not sleep well, or even get to bed later, but your days begin early, so this leaves you exhausted. If you stick to a routine and use your time wisely you may be able to plan your day better and remove the extra anxiety you are putting on yourself. And add time in there for you to rest, so that you can keep your body and mind strong. A little exercise, even a walk would be good too.

Remember that it is not just the caregiving role that you are doing. You also have food to make and groceries to pick up. Not to mention, that maybe you are working at home or have other family members you need to take care of, so you really do need to plan your day. Add in some extra time for interruptions or things that may not go right. You will be glad you did.

When you are organized, you can easily stay on top of appointments and events and keep the chaos down. If you have a day where things are just not going as smoothly, it is easier to catch up on one day, than two or three. That in turn can remove a lot of stress and give you better control of your life instead of feeling lost. As a caregiver, you have enough to worry about without wondering where that important paper or email was filed away. You can organize your day and your tasks according to a routine which will help you be in better control of things.

Being late for appointments, missing them, or showing up at the incorrect times can cost you some grief. You can even miss important payments because you were not sure of the payment dates, or you just didn't take the time to pay them or set up an automatic withdrawal with your bank. That can easily get you in trouble with your credit. The paperwork for due dates can be buried deep amongst other papers or a bunch of emails not opened, because they were mixed in with other stuff. Things can get missed even with the technology we have available to us today. You still need some time to organize things and minimize anxiety.

You can easily split important papers or emails from the not-so-important ones. File papers or emails away alphabetically, or under their names, or whatever way works for you that allows you to locate what you need quickly. Even using various programs to advise you of due dates for payments or important expiry dates of items you may have. Or contracts that are ending and you must contact the company before the expiry dates.

I know many like to go paperless, but for me, I like to have a small filing area, so that things stay neat and I can locate what I need quickly. I don't always trust technology when it comes to those important papers and let's face it, there are papers you do need the original of. I even make copies of some important contracts or receipts because I found that the ink from many of those bills these days, fades away and things can get lost electronically too. When you are handling your affairs plus those of a loved one, it's even more important to stay organized as you don't want to mix both things up.

When your place is organized, your brain feels organized and when you are looking for things, you remember where they are as well as can locate them quickly. You don't have to waste time looking for something. And when you have company coming, you don't have to run around cleaning your place up, because most things will be in order. At least that's the goal.

For someone like my ex-husband who suffered from Bipolar, not finding what he needed right away would frustrate him more than the average person. He would get angry at himself for misplacing something or missing an appointment, which could lead him to an emotional decline. When he was able to locate what he needed or was on time for an appointment, he felt more in control of his environment, and this minimized his emotional ups and downs. He also did not have to rebook those missed appointments that can be costly.

When attending those doctor appointments, you want to know you have the correct date and time as well as bring along any paperwork you need to take with you. Sometimes that paperwork can be important, and you don't want to spend time looking for it or have to fill out everything again. Especially if it took a while to do.

Prepare anything you need to take with you ahead of time, like any medications, or taking a list of what they are. Most pharmacies can print you that list, so you don't have to take everything with you. There were countless times I would attend appointments with my parents, and I always had the information ready ahead of time, so I could ensure I would not forget anything. And even today, I take a list of their medical history with me, so that if the doctors ask me something, like an exact date of an ailment or surgery or whatever they may need, I can just refer to my information.

This was very important when my ill parent had their major health crisis. I was the one that headed to the hospital in the ambulance with them. The ambulance attendant asked me many questions and I was able to answer most of them since I know their medical history, but anything else I could not remember because I was so frazzled, I was able to go to my notes. After we got my ill parent home, it was even more important to stay organized with their health records, especially so when there were several other times, we ended up back in an ambulance and specific dates and information were vitally important. I even kept a picture of their health cards with me on my phone, so that if my other parent lost the card or it was not with us, I had a copy, which was good enough for the attendants.

Along with the extra duties we had to care for them, we had to keep their medications in order, in stock, and administering them on time. If we had repeat prescriptions at the pharmacy, we had to call ahead of time, so they could prepare them all. Plus, we had them packaged, so it took time to put them together. We had to make sure the doctor was available for house calls before we ran out of medications, so we had to stay on top of all of this. Do you want to talk about being organized? We had to indeed be on our toes.

It was vital to also have the day organized for my ill parent so that we did not miss anything. Clean clothes were needed, so we had to ensure the laundry got done often. We had to get up and get my ill parent ready for the morning before the PSW's came to do their thing, so we had to make sure my ill parent had breakfast early. Then we had to organize the different medications and depending on the number of people that had to come, like therapists or the workers' supervisors I had to make sure I was ready for them too, with the information they needed. Or have my parent in or out of bed and into their wheelchair, so there may have been some coordination involved. Sometimes it would be noon before I would even be able to stop for breakfast when most were ready for lunch. So, there was a lot of preparation.

Staying organized helps the entire family to be on the same page. Everybody knows what is going on when and where. It takes the guesswork out of who is taking on a task or leaving it for someone else. Especially, when there is more than one person taking care of someone. You have to make sure you each know who is taking on what task and who has the important paperwork. If this sounds like having good communication, the two do not work far from each other.

It's not a bad idea to split the responsibilities with others that are helping to care for your loved ones. Otherwise, everyone will end up pointing fingers at everybody else when a task is not done. If you are caring for the elderly who cannot take care of their affairs any longer, for example, and multiple children are looking after them, give the one responsibility of organizing finances to the person that is best equipped to handle this. That way all the important payments are not missed. Give the other siblings another task and then communicate with each other where you are at, so you all know what is going on and can work together on things. I know it's not so cut a dry but striving towards your goal of keeping things in order will certainly take some pressure off everyone. And if you lose track of things, just do your best to get back in line and organized again.

Keeping everything in order also cuts down on everybody bugging you for anything they may be looking for. There is usually one parent in the household that knows where everything is, down to the exact spot like, 'top shelf, left-hand side, behind the milk', kind of description, and that was me. I know where most things are and rarely can I not find something. Not to say it does not happen of course, but rarely.

When I was dealing with my ex-husband, we did not use our phones as we do today, with information at our fingertips and alerts to remind us of certain things. If you are comfortable leaving reminders on your phones make sure you set things up well, so that you see or hear the reminder, like when it is time to take medication. And also remember to check your phone to make sure it is not placed on silent, or the volume turned down, or the phone off, because you may not get the messages or alerts you are looking for in time.

I still like to use a calendar or planner today to organize things, splitting up important tasks or events. Sometimes I put papers in folders and put them in a specific order and organize them, so I know where to find them. Especially, when it comes to my writing since I have different projects I like to work on. I don't need everything out, but when I need information, I want it handy. I will know where to go to find it. And make sure when you save things on your computer, you know where you are putting things because it can be a bottomless pit to find something in the land of electronics.

My ex-husband's exasperation of finding things was minimized with things a little more organized. The towels went in one spot, the bandages were in another, extra toothpaste was always found in the supply area for bathroom products, and so on. Even today, I try and arrange my space the same, like in the kitchen cupboards, closets, and more so that we can find things quickly. And when I change it I can't find what I'm looking for.

It helps to know when you need to order supplies if you are organized because you may have a specific day to order items since you know roughly how long an item lasts like paper towels, for example. Or know when something needs replacing since everything is in the same spot or organized in whatever way works for you that you can easily identify what needs to be purchased. And if you order certain items on occasion, keep a list of the name of what it is or a picture, so that you know exactly what you are looking for next time.

Not everyone will work the same way of course, but these are just some of the things I do to help me stay organized, and if there is something I need it's usually where I know it's going to be. Not to say that I do not move things around from time to time and change things up, but I generally stick to the same way. So, you have to find what works for you and your family and also what minimizes everybody interrupting you when they want something now. It can get nerve-racking when three or four different people come looking for you because they can't find something and you are in the middle of something else, or maybe even wanting that downtime you have been craving.

This has come in handy many times, but the one time that comes to mind presently, was the following day after my ill parent was rushed to the hospital. We had been at a family function when my parent fell ill. We all ended up at the hospital for several days, still in our good clothes. I was in high heels for over 24 hours, and they were not shoes, comfortable enough to be in them for that long. Let's face it, even the most comfortable shoes are uncomfortable after wearing them for 24 hours straight. When I sent my kid home to pick up a change of clothing for me, I was able to tell them where to find what I wanted, because I knew where the items would be. And my kid also knew where some of those items were, like runners or extra toothbrushes.

My kid, who I adore, often tells me, "I have that mom's brain," and know where everything is, even if they have misplaced things. Yes, I accept, I have that mom's brain and remember for the most part, where I put things, but another reason why I know where to find the things I am looking for is that they usually are in the same place. Like apples will usually go on one side of the fridge, and eggs in another spot and I try and keep to that, so everyone knows where to find what they are looking for, not to mention save food from being thrown out when it gets pushed to the back of the fridge and you forgot it was there. And the reason why I can find my kid's things is that I know their organizational style. Only so many places I know they will put down the keys. Ah, the joys of being a mom.

When it came to organizing things while taking care of my ill parent it was easier for us as well as for the PSW's that were coming and going to help us. We moved two dressers into the new space where my ill parent would make their new room and filled them with all the necessary items needed for their care, like clothes, washcloths, and other items. We kept things in the same drawers each time we put them away, and I labeled them for the caregiver's sake. That way if someone different would come in, they just had to read the labels. It was easier for my other healthier parent to find things as well and cut down on the confusion of trying to locate something we needed immediately. Emotions were already heightened, so it helped to keep others calmer.

I remember trying to find the blow dryer once to dry my ill parent's hair and no matter where we looked, we could not locate it. Because I lived there, it was not a problem. I simply grabbed mine, but by the time I had come back upstairs, my parent was already shivering from having their hair wet. It turned out that one of the PSW's had put the blow dryer in a box with seasonal blankets, so we did not bother to search there. The PSW did not mention what she had done, and it took us a while to find the blow-dryer since we had moved various boxes around to keep the room tidy.

My healthier parent had become upset when we could not find the blow-dryer, thinking someone had taken it. This is another thing I just want to add. It was an old blow dryer. If it had gone missing, then I figured it was time for another one. I did not allow this type of event to bother me. There were bigger issues to worry about.

Stay organized and it will take a load of pressure off your day, so you can concentrate on more important things. When you don't have a lot of time on your hands you want to minimize your stress levels so the more organized you are the smoother your days will go.

Chapter Nine

Simple Step Number 8

Take Time For You

As I have said repeatedly, we always forget to take care of ourselves, and the next thing we know, we are sick too. It is especially important to take time for us because as I found out the hard way, ailments will creep up on you, and then it can be too late to rewind your health. Because I stayed fit, my body was strong, and I kept beating up on it as I cared for everyone else. Not only was my body feeling the stress, the lack of sleep, but my brain was handling a lot at one time, only to have to handle more as life continued.

There was so much I wanted to do still in my life, and everything was put on hold. I had my children's story I had wanted to write for a lifetime and finally did. I also wanted to share my experiences and hope they could better someone else's life. I hoped to find another partner and maybe even marry again. There were things I wanted to learn and continue to better myself, maybe learn how to paint or draw, which I loved to dabble with. Maybe go on a trip somewhere warm with some friends and enjoy another part of the world. But I could not do any of those things. I was too busy taking care of everyone else to worry about my career or doing what made me happy. It could have just been to take a day off and visit a friend, have a massage, soak in the tube, but my time was not my own. I know, I only had myself to blame for that.

When I looked in the mirror one day, I realized how tired I looked and how beat up my body felt. I had bags under my eyes, and lines on my forehead I swore neither one of them was there before. I have a lot of hair and it's curly and wavey and frizzy and does its own thing and if I do not manage it, I look like I just woke up out of bed, and believe me, it can look crazy.

Where before I would be impeccable with the way I looked and dressed, I did not have time to look after myself as I cared for my loved ones. I was too exhausted and there wasn't' enough time. I kept my hair long and would usually pull it back because it was easier and faster to care for as I still wanted to look somewhat put together, but I ended up cutting it short, hoping I did not have to bother with it as much. I still don't know which way is easier. I was not one to put a lot of make-up on, but as I said, I always liked to look nice.

When I was caring for my ill parent, I actually left the house without any makeup on at all, not even eyeliner, or lipstick and I would leave the house in track pants and running shoes, which I also never did. But I could not bother to pretty myself up or change my clothes. What was the use? I would have to come home and change again and remove the makeup and I was too exhausted to care or go through the motions of changing so many times.

Now, I know, many people leave the house dressed this way, but for me, that was out of the ordinary. It was my, 'at home', relaxed look, not my going out, look and it even shocked my kid who was surprised at me leaving the house in tracks and runners the first time. I guess we all have to change at some point in our lives.

I was holding myself back from living my life the way I wanted to. But I accepted it as my duty to look after the people that were put in my life. The universe I guess thought I was the best person to care for these people I love and so here I was doing that job. Looking after their physical and mental well-being.

But what about our own needs? Just because we are in this role, does not mean we can't enjoy our own lives. Either you continue to see the situation through, maybe at the expense of your health or you begin to live your life too. I am not saying you just get up and leave your loved one to fend for themselves but stop and do something for yourself. Reach out to others to give you a hand. Set your boundaries and stick to them. It will make every day you live that much better, and happier. In turn, it will make others around you feel better too because if you are happy, they will be too. And they know the sacrifices you are taking to be the one looking after them.

I felt that the universe had chosen me for this special job, and I was honored to be the one to do it. I was happy to love them, happy to care for them, honored I was picked for such a special task of loving someone so much, but we can never lose ourselves in what we are doing. We still have our own lives to live. Funny how the universe puts us in the places we need to be, either to learn a lesson, prepare us for something bigger, or because we are chosen for another reason.

Remember to always love yourself as much as you love your loved ones. Also, remember you are so important because if you were not on this earth doing what you are doing so many people would suffer. We are a special breed that can manage to do this work and do it well, with so much love in our hearts. We are the chosen ones, so to speak. Chosen for the qualities we have, whether they are loving ones or tough ones meant to teach someone a lesson. So, if you find yourself in the caregiving role, know how truly special you are. The Universe is looking down on you smiling and thanking you for your love.

Chapter Ten

In Closing

Never Lose Sight

Never lose sight of who you are, what your goals are, and what you wish to accomplish in this life. We may have some curveballs sent our way and maybe change course but remember to pick yourself back up and drive in the direction you wish to steer your life. Call on others to help you through it, especially on tough days. Learn about the ailments your loved ones have, but also learn about yourself and what makes you happy.

Find music that makes you dance or put on some television shows that make you laugh and get you out of a slump. Prioritize your time so you can fit things in that you want to do. Do not do it all alone, because climbing that mountain on your own can be hard.

For me, I would meditate when things got difficult. I could not just leave a situation on the spot, but I would sit on my bed at the end of the day, even as exhausted as I was and take a moment. I would read or listen to music. I found the 432 hertz calmed me and would look for other soothing music, like sound baths, which are the sounds from crystal bowls being played. I looked for different healing modalities that helped me to center myself and heal my body. Body Talk, Reiki, Tapping, and other forms. I even got my crystals out which I love to know and learn about and meditated with my special candles, scented candles, or incense.

I have made the most amazing friends in my journey to heal what I thought was broken. My heart, my spirit, but they were not broken, just afraid to get hurt again. I just had to trust in the love I had all around me that I could not see because I was so busy being busy. I went for walks in nature and marveled even more than I used to before at the beauty all around us.

The way the trees and flowers grew and bloomed, giving off such fragrance, blessing us with thier beauty. Gardeners ready to plant their seeds and enjoying the magic of what would grow into the summer months. Even the winter days were wonderful because I knew there would soon be snow falling. An excitement that would have me calling my mother the minute I would see it fall. Memories of my childhood and the fun we would have as we played in it. Friendly snowball fights and angle designs as we fell backwards, our arms opened wide, knowing the snow would soften our fall. We could feel the cold on our skin as the snow would find it's way inside our mittens or boots. But we didn't care. It was just too much fun!

As awful as it can be when driving and as cold as it can get here in Canada, just take a moment after a snowfall, and look around at the wonder and beauty. The trees are full of white glistening snow and just everything that goes with it. Skiing, skating, tobogganing, hearing laughter as kids come down a hill with their sleds. And look at the wonder of nature as you see how waterfalls are frozen in time or the leaves on the trees change in the fall.

We get so lost in what we are going through sometimes, that we forget the world is still spinning all around us and we can enjoy it in different ways. Situations may not always be easy, and we may feel like we may never get out of the hole we are in, but it is up to us to stay strong and learn how to enjoy what we have in front of us. It is also up to us to free ourselves from the things that are holding us back from experiencing life. Release old ways that no longer serve you. Re-invent yourself if you have to but find yourself again if you are lost.

We live in a world of technology that is full of information helping us in so many ways and even if you do not have any technology to help you, reach out a hand and someone will be there to help. Ask for it, do not remain silent, accepting what you see in front of you. Open your mind and your heart.

It pained me to have to leave my ex-husband. I loved him very much and was concerned for his well-being, but circumstances did not permit us to stay with him, so we left to continue to stay alive and live. From that union, as difficult as it could be, I not only met a beautiful man that I loved and had some wonderful years together, but I gained a wonderful extended family in knowing him. We made a beautiful child together that was conceived out of deep love. I have the privilege of being a big part of that life every day and have been able to watch them grow into the wonderful adult they are now. I am a proud mother and they put a smile on my face every day I look their way. I love the things they do and say, and they keep me strong and keep me going. Had I lost myself in my caregiving roles, I may not have been around to see the beauty I have in my life. Or maybe I would have made myself so ill, that I could not appreciate it all.

Taking care of my parents allowed me to spend time with them and give them my love and affection. Our bond only grew from that time spent together. I learned more about myself and what I am capable of. I also learned that I was living a life for everyone else and forgot to live mine. I had to change things around and make some difficult choices, but those choices have brought me to today and I am glad I did not stay stagnant.

I did lose sight of where I was going a long time ago, but I had to pick myself off the ground several times to keep going. I had to gain confidence in myself and most of all I had to learn to love myself, as much as I love those around me. It was not uncommon to look around my room and find sticky notes of encouragement or beside my desk and in the bathroom. I had to look hard at the woman that looked back at me in the mirror and find where she was, pull her out and live life.

While I was cleaning one day, I came across some of my younger pictures of me as a little girl. As I looked at my face, I saw the smile. I was always smiling, always willing to give a hand to someone else. I was full of hope, wonder, and love. I had to get back to those feelings as the adult. I had to leave the experiences from the past, in the past. Yes, they have shaped me, but I no longer needed those experiences to move into the future.

Love is all around us. We just need to find it in us first. Then share it. Never lose sight of the love you have for yourselves.

Love always,

S R John

Journal/Notes

Use the next several pages to journal your day, add your thoughts or release anything you wish to get off your chest. Maybe you didn't speak up for yourself during a conversation, or maybe you did, and it didn't go as you had hoped. Or you pushed through your day and are finally relaxing.

We must thrive to give ourselves some love. We all have challenges and people who depend on us. Sometimes we do things because it's expected of us in our culture, in our lives, and because of the beliefs that hold us hostage.

Most times it's out of love. We have choices. Some are hard and will have repercussions. It just takes loving us to step into our power and take charge of our life and make it all work. Stay strong, love yourself, and be brave. And if you fall back down, get back up and work at loving yourself all over again. I'm sure you will find you become stronger with each setback, learning, and growing to be who You want to be and the way you wish to shape your life.

Journal/Notes

Journal/Notes

Journal/Notes

Thank You For Reading!

I hope this book has helped you in some small way. It is through working and learning together that we can all make a difference in our world.

Please add a review on Amazon and let me know what you thought!

Amazon reviews are very helpful for authors. Thank you for taking the time to support me and my work. Don't forget to share your reviews on social media with the hashtag bipolarlovesrjohn

About The Author

Sebastiana R. John lives in Canada with her family. She has experienced being a caregiver firsthand, first with her ex-husband who was diagnosed with Bipolar and then while caring for an ill parent. There are lessons that we can all learn from each other on taking care of those we love without losing ourselves in the process.

srjohn2018@gmail.com

srjohn@bell.net

Facebook page: bipolarlovesrjohn
Facebook Page: srjohnofficial

Other Books by S. R. John
Ghost Detective The Magic Ruby – Fiction now on Amazon

https://www.amazon.ca/Ghost-Detective-Magic-Ruby-John/dp/1999424514

Look out for another upcoming book:
Bipolar Love Experiencing Mental Illness
From The Other Side

www.ingramcontent.com/pod-product-compliance
Lightning Source LLC
LaVergne TN
LVHW050642100826
845148LV00011B/1946